M000316973

# SNOW GLOBE
# LEADERSHIP
## SHAKEN NOT SETTLED

### BEST SELLING AUTHOR
## JEFF NISCHWITZ

Copyright © 2021 by NOW SC Press

All rights reserved. No part of this publication may be reproduced, distributed, or transmitted in any form or by any means, including photocopying, recording, or other electronic or mechanical methods, without the prior written permission of the publisher, except in the case of brief quotations embodied in critical reviews and certain other noncommercial uses permitted by copyright law. For permission requests, write to the publisher, addressed "Attention: Permissions Coordinator," via the website below.

Publish@nowscpress.com
www.PublishWithNOW.com
@nowscpress

Ordering Information:

Quantity sales. Special discounts are available on quantity purchases by corporations, associations, and others. For details, contact the publisher at the address above.

Orders by U.S. trade bookstores and wholesalers. Please contact: NOW SC Press: Tel: (813) 970-8470 or visit www.PublishWithNOW.com

Printed in the United States of America

First Printing 2021

ISBN: 978-1-7369388-3-6

# Praise for *Snow Globe Leadership*

"I love the metaphor in Snow Globe Leadership, Shaken Not Settled. Jeff teaches us that the real magic in life and in our organizations is in the shaking - not staying stagnant and content but pushing ourselves to constantly view our relationships and ourselves differently. Read this book and sprinkle some of this magic on those that you love and serve."

*Tommy Spaulding, New York Times Bestselling Author of*
*The Gift of Influence and The Heart-Led Leader*

"Jeff Nischwitz makes a brilliant case for shaking things up in his new book, *Snow Globe Leadership*. Since we've all experienced months of uncertainty, worry and constant pivots, the timing for his book couldn't be better. He shares substantive commentary on why today's leaders need to adjust the way they think and work. He also offers some satisfying strategies for determining where to start and how to reap the benefits of constant personal and professional evolution. I look forward to recommending this book to leaders who are ready to shake things up and transform their potential for success."

*Sara Canaday, Leadership Expert, Keynote Speaker &*
*Award-Winning Author (www.SaraCanaday.com)*

"We're navigating challenging times and changes in business that demand a new approach to leadership, and Jeff Nischwitz's *Snow Globe Leadership* delivers just the leadership disruption we need. Much like the shifts offered in my book *Transfluence,* Jeff encourages leaders to embrace vulnerability, authenticity and empathy as leadership superpowers in order to build trust, nurture cultures and grow businesses.

*Walter Rakowich, Business Leader, Former CEO of*
*Prologis & Author of Transfluence: How to Lead with*
*Transformative Influence in Today's Climates of Change*

"Jeff encapsulates the simple into the profound by making snow globes the perfect metaphor for one's own leadership "shake ups". He boldly invites leaders to assess their organization's tolerance factor and declares that what and who an organization tolerates, in fact, becomes the culture. A must read for leaders and aspiring leaders."

*Deana Labriola, Partner, Fox Rothschild LLP*

"In your hands you hold the new guide for leading in a time of tremendous change and challenge. There has never been a better time to take the best of what go you to this moment, apply this wisdom and become the leader you were always meant to be. Adding *just one step* consistently over the course of your year will transform your culture and elevate your influence."

*Mark LeBlanc, CSP, Author of*
*Never Be the Same and Rainmaker Confidential*

"'*Transformation requires* **both** *shaking and shifting.*' These words are some of the most foundational when speaking of leadership and building culture, and Jeff Nischwitz has intentionally zeroed in on them in this book with zeal, sophistication and good, old common sense. We need transformed leaders, not band-aid leaders. In *Snow Globe Leadership*, Jeff gives new meaning to the concept of disruption, and invites us to be leaders of our own lives, first, in order to truly and properly understand the power, significance and necessary approach to leading others."

*Traci Philips, Founder of The Innate Coach - Executive Leadership &*
*Performance Coaching for Visionaries and Author of Looking IN:*
*Discover, Define & Align the True Value of Your Life, Leadership & Legacy*

"Two of Jeff's many talents intersect in this transformational leadership tour de force: first, his ability to diagnose the root causes of challenges we face as leaders, and second, his gift of communicating a powerful alternative approach in clear, immediately actionable language. Every conversation I have with Jeff makes me a better father, husband, leader, and person – *Snow Globe Leadership, Shaken Not Settled* is 1,000 of those highly impactful conversations condensed into one. Caution: read only if you are ready to be Jeffed."

*David J. Akers, Executive Vice President, Equalis Group*

"I read about 30 business books a year, and if I can get 1-2 nuggets out of each one, I consider it a win. This book did not disappoint. Jeff's in-your-face, direct approach called me out on several things and made me think differently. One big takeaway is not saying 'don't take this personally' because we wouldn't say that before complimenting!"

*Marcey Rader, Chief Productivity Lead, Rader Co.*

"In *Snow Globe Leadership*, his newest book, Jeff Nischwitz uses the metaphor of the snow globe to encourage us to both shake up and then to shift our worlds. Why? For bigger impact and more positive outcomes. He urges us to ask deeper, more probing questions of ourselves and those we love and care for to move us toward more wholeness, joy and fulfillment in leadership and life. *Snow Globe Leadership* empowers you to see—and experience—more of the beauty in your life when you learn to do the shaking."

*Michael Malone, University of Miami, Director of Editorial Services*

"Controversially, this book turns traditional leadership styles on their heads and challenges the reader to be brave, take risks and be intuitively vulnerable in those moments that really matter. From spotting your gaps, blinds spots or 'tolerance factor' to finding out how to take your leadership to the next level – whatever stage you're at in your leadership journey, there's something for you to take away, improve upon and ultimately master to become that great leader you always knew you had it in you to be."

*Leona Donaghy, Founder, Wholehearted Environments*

"Snow Globe Leadership could be Jeff's finest book yet. All of the topics are so relevant for both our personal and professional lives; especially post pandemic times. I have learned a great deal from understanding and embracing what Jeff calls *The Tolerance Factor*. His well thought out assessment tool has helped me to ask tough questions to better understand where I might be stagnant at home or at work. The ultimate goal is to shake things up for continuous growth, development and improvement in all areas of our lives."

*Amy Johnson, Brookfield Properties,*
*IT Business Relationship Manager*

# Dedication

During many conversations and podcast interviews over the past couple of years, I'm often asked about leadership thought-leaders that I follow and about who has influenced my work. I struggle with this answer because there are so many, but a few regularly come to mind including Tommy Spaulding, Walt Rakowich, Brene Brown and Simon Sinek.

In these conversations, I'm also asked about leadership mentors, and this list is markedly shorter. In fact, the person who regularly comes to mind when asked about leadership mentors is my Dad, Ron Nischwitz. I've watched my Dad lead and coach for most of my life, but often from a distance. As an entrepreneur and business owner, my Dad built a highly successful business, transitioned the management to others and ultimately sold the business. As a Division I baseball coach for 30 years (Wright State University), my Dad built a nationally known baseball program, won many games and honors, helped birth a couple of major league careers and most importantly, inspired, mentored, coached and impacted hundreds of young men. He also founded a non-profit that helped teach and inspire teen entrepreneurs and business leaders (Ohio Business Week). And of course, he was actively involved in leadership with many business organizations and industry associations.

Universally, my Dad is admired, respected and remembered by the people he impacted throughout his experiences, and certainly he's led an impactful life.

Over recent years, my Dad and I have spent a lot more time together and certainly have talked more than we did most of our lives. During those experiences and conversations, I've realized that many of the leadership seeds planted in me were planted by my Dad. There are many, but the ones that most come to mind are perseverance, humility, relationship building, trusting others and empowering people. One big one is modeling and work ethic—as a coach, Dad's players often "hated" that for most of his coaching career he never asked them to do anything that he wasn't willing to do himself. Whether it was doing large numbers of push-ups and sit-ups, doing long-distance runs or gutting out outfield sprints, Dad worked as hard, if not harder, than his players. He also put this energy into his business and other ventures. I know that Dad's work ethic came from his father (my grandfather), but I'll limit this dedication to a single generation.

Thanks Dad for planting so many amazing leadership seeds in me and the world!

# Contents

# Foreword

This book is an essential contribution at a time of great disruption and self-awareness. We face a critical leadership gap in business and society today. It's tempting to play it safe, anchoring ourselves to our identity and who we *were* as leaders to feel comfortable. However, this does not propel us forward. We need to address the leadership gap and "shake-up our snow globes" as the intentional and committed leaders we aspire to be.

Jeff Nischwitz's book will definitely "shake your snow globe" and inspire you to shake your own. This is a book that should be well thumbed, highlighted and annotated with notes in the margins. Having read it over two days and having made many pages of notes, Jeff provides us all with practical and foundational perspective shifts, examples, stories, tools and tips. He helps us all to shift our mindsets to enhance, empower and energise our leadership and our leadership impact.

If you aspire to inspire as a leader, then this book's for you. However, Health Warning: don't read this book if you're not prepared to shake your own leadership globe! It will make you feel deeply uncomfortable, as you realise there is much work for you to do. Jeff Nischwitz's insightful tools and techniques will make you feel disrupted, challenging you to define and perhaps redefine the leader you aspire to be

The journey highlights the importance of trust in leadership and how it creates strong cultures, where influence is built and impact is created. "Time to get naked" stresses the importance of appropriate vulnerability by us as leaders. This is followed naturally by cultures of psychological safety and the benefits that flow from them. Next Jeff helps us to identify our blind spots and become even more self-aware in order to navigate and address them.

A critical theme and chapter of the book is the power of being fully present and the gift your presence has on attention, intention, energy and commitment. Making leadership all about others, not being selfish and using the power of silence will remain with us as bits of wise advice. As a couple we'll now ask ourselves, "Am I present?" We'll take the challenge further and ask each other, "Are you present?" Jeff's advice on holding ourselves accountable and having the courage to encourage feedback cultures are timely reminders to all leaders.

Another profound theme is about our impact, attention, intention, responsibility and awareness. Therefore, servant leadership and personal modeling are critical. This in turn leads to Jeff's profound work on the "tolerance factor." His words should be written over the door of every business: "Our leadership, culture and impact are not defined by what we preach, but by what and who we tolerate." In our own coaching and development work with leaders around the world, this is truly insightful.

We have both had the pleasure of getting to know Jeff and personally experience his essential leadership and character traits of authenticity, courage and compassion. Only the strong can be vulnerable and his transformational work on "Be a Man," the "Daily Shake Up" and the "Leadership Junkies Podcast" means that "Getting Jeffed" will make you think more deeply than ever before and inspire you into action.

Of the over 200 books that we've read, analysed, reviewed and drawn crucial lessons from to put into practice in the last three years, this is now one of our favourites. Undoubtedly. Jeff is right when he claims that leadership is broken in so many areas and needs a new people centric culture of real psychological safety.

As leaders we need to exhibit and earn in return more humanity, vulnerability, trust and relationship building. This is where Jeff's essential disruption and snow globe shake ups are needed. Read, absorb and answer his call to action, his call to humanity, his call to leadership.

*Leigh and Jonathan Bowman-Perks MBE*
*Global Leadership Coaches to Chairs, CEOs and Executive Boards*
*Top 1.5% of Global Broadcasters, Entrepreneur & Team Coaches*
*Inspiring Leadership International Ltd*

# Chapter 1

# Shaking Up
# Your Leadership

I was speaking on a stage in Raleigh, NC in 2017 when the thought hit me—snow globes. I'd never thought about snow globes before, didn't own a snow globe and certainly had never seen them as a profound metaphor for leadership and life. But I trusted the message that came to me on the stage that day and this idea—the importance of shaking things up—has grown deeper and become more integrated into my leadership, life and work.

We all know about snow globes and they all have many things in common. First, they're generally round—thus, we call them snow *globes*. Second, they offer some idyllic scenes, whether it be a building, a skyline, a mountain view, a farmscape, a holiday scene or even a beach. While there are differences—some are glass and some are plastic, some are light and some are heavy, some have music and others don't, some contain white snow and others contain sparkling snow—they all have one significant thing in common: *the magic only happens when you shake it.*

Indeed, snow globes are made to be shaken, and without shaking them, they're just another pretty piece that sits on your shelf, desk or table. In my travels, I've discovered that even though we all know the magic of snow globes, few of us ever shake our snow globes because they're pretty enough as they are. Beyond this literal truth about snow globes, they have several powerful lessons to teach us about leadership and life. This book is your invitation to become a fully committed snow globe shaker and leader.

## The Magic Is in the Shaking

What I've come to deeply understand and experience is that what's true for snow globes is also true of your leadership, relationships and lives—*it's critical that you regularly shake your snow globe.* While looking good is nice, the snow globe's magic is in the shaking, and this is also true for every element of your leadership. In fact, a snow globe at rest is like your life at rest—*it looks good, but there's not much happening.* While you may think that a snow globe and life at rest are peaceful, the reality is that they're just settled. In fact, an apt description of a snow globe at rest is that it's not living up to its potential or what it was built to be and experience. The same is true for you and your leadership—without regular shaking, it's just okay and you're not living up to all you were built to be, experience and impact. And that's just it— impact is the objective of leadership.

*Impact is the objective of leadership.*

To be clear, I'm not suggesting that change for the sake of change is a good thing, but a snow globe isn't about change. No matter how much you shake a snow globe, it doesn't change its essence—you only see things differently for a short period of time while the snow or sparkles are swirling. No, the shaking isn't the change—the shaking is designed to give you a new and different perspective about a situation, a challenge, an opportunity, a person, a relationship and even yourself.

With this shaken perspective you can then decide what (if any) changes to make in your beliefs, actions or both.

## SHAKE REGULARLY

Another lesson that I've learned is that no matter how long or how often you shake a snow globe, things quickly go back to normal, and this is a typical form of settling for many of us. Because snow globes are designed to look good even without the magic of shaking, as soon as you stop shaking them they quickly *settle* into being just a nice-looking display piece. Similarly, when you shake things up in your leadership, your team, your organization or your life, you feel the magic, but it's fleeting and things quickly go back to the way they were before. In other words, *they settle into what's comfortable.*

We all know that it's easy to live comfortably in every aspect of our lives, and it's also easy to quickly revert back to the old normal (your comfort zones) after a brief shake-up. Perhaps you've read a book that filled you with new approaches and ideas. You might even have tried out some of these new actions for a brief time, but you quickly fell back to your old and comfortable ways. Perhaps you attended some training program and left it feeling on fire and ready to change the world (the shake-up), but then came everyday life, demands and distractions, and you ended up almost where you were before anything was shaken. This is why regularly shaking your leadership and life snow globe is so essential—to help you sustain and expand the momentum so you can achieve real and lasting change in thinking, actions and outcomes.

Not only is it critical to regularly shake up your snow globe but shaking your own snow globe is a fantastic act of modeling for everyone around you. Whether it's your partner, your family or your team, your act of snow globe shaking encourages and invites others to do the same. In addition, in any role where you can have a leadership impact, you can encourage others to shake their snow globes and make it safe for them to shake. In fact, you can even shake their snow globes for them in many ways.

One of the best ways to shake up the snow globes of the people you care about is to ask questions. High-quality and authentic questions serve us well in shaking our own snow globes and those of the people around us. Questions invite self-assessment, grow self-awareness, encourage personal responsibility and empower others to self-shake, self-shift and self-accelerate. While it's ultimately up to another person whether they actually change (yes, it's true—you can't change someone else), we all have the opportunity to shake other people's snow globes in various aspects of their lives. While there's always risk associated with the shaking, whether you're shaking your own snow globe or someone else's, that's the nature of personal and professional leadership. After all, nobody said that shaking things up was easy or risk free.

## MUST SHAKE AND SHIFT

One thing we know about snow globes and change is that shaking and disruption alone are not enough. No matter how often or how vigorously you shake your personal snow globe or your organizational snow globe, nothing changes from the shaking alone. In fact, that's the big problem with most change initiatives—lots of shaking but too little shifting—because the shaking alone doesn't create the shifts that create change and impact.

Think about the snow globe—you shake it vigorously and you witness the magic, but as soon as you stop shaking everything immediately starts to settle and nothing has fundamentally changed inside the globe. Yes, the snow or sparkles have all relocated but the foundation (whatever's inside) hasn't changed. This is where shifting comes into play.

*Shaking alone doesn't create the shifts that create change and impact.*

When you shake things up you must also make fundamental shifts in your perspectives and actions, because these shifts are what influence different outcomes and impact. The same is true with your team. Too often leaders create lots of shaking but there are no accompanying shifts that create impact and change outcome. Instead, everyone feels shaken up but without any new outcomes, which makes people uncertain and fearful, rather than inspired, empowered and encouraged. Just remember this snow globe leadership truth—*transformation requires **both** shaking and shifting.*

I've now shared this message from hundreds of stages and with thousands of people over the past few years, and this book is the next step in sharing this impactful wisdom with the world. I've also become enthralled with snow globes, collecting them whenever I travel to a new place—my collection now includes more than fifty (50) snow globes. My hope is that you'll fully embrace and embody snow globe shaking in your leadership and life, and I know you'll quickly experience the transformation that follows from snow globe shaking and the shifts you make while shaking.

## Watch Over Your Snow Globe

My friend Robin Sacks wrote a wonderful book called *Get Off My Bus!: How to Get Clarity, Get in the Driver's Seat, and Get Moving in Your Life!* (Outskirts 2010), which encourages us all to get certain people off of our life bus. In other words, stop letting yourself be surrounded by the people who discourage you, deplete you and get in your way. It's a simple and profound concept—getting people off your bus—and I recently realized that when you kick them off your bus you've got to do one more thing. You have to take back your snow globe.

If you're wondering how the hell these other people got their hands on *your snow globe*, the answer is simple and sad—*you gave it to them!* Yes, you heard me right—you've given your snow globe to other people, and most of you have also surrendered it to the vagaries of circumstances. By the way, in nearly every case you didn't consciously or intentionally give up your snow globe, but you did give it up.

Sometimes we give up our snow globes because we want to avoid personal responsibility for our lives and our outcomes. Sometimes we give them up because we're afraid. Sometimes we give them up because we're simply tired of being responsible. Many times we give up our snow globes to the people closest to us either because they asked us for them (usually unconsciously) or we believe that handing over our snow globes to someone else is an act of love or an investment in the relationship.

No matter what the cause or circumstances of you giving up and handing over your snow globe, it's time to reclaim your snow globe and to take personal responsibility for it and for its shaking.

## SHAKING THROUGH DISRUPTION

Given my embrace of the snow globe metaphor for leadership, it's not surprising that this quote from Netflix Co-Founder Marc Randolph showed up a few years ago and now is featured in my email signature: "You have to disrupt yourself, before someone disrupts you." Certainly Netflix knows a few things about disruption, and the COVID pandemic gave us a new twist: *You have to disrupt yourself before **something** else does.* This brings up a natural question that I've been asked dozens of times during the past year—With all the disruption happening around me and to me, do I really need to keep shaking things up? My answer is an emphatic YES!

When you're getting shaken up by life and circumstances, it's natural to feel like you can take a break on shaking your own leadership and life snow globe. However, while the instinct is natural, the opposite is true—when you're being externally disrupted, internal disruption (and snow globe shaking) is even more vital. Think of this way … imagine that you're inside a large snow globe and you're being vigorously shaken by external circumstances. You try to stand firm and hang on, but the truth is you'll be thrown around and slammed against the walls of the globe because it's impossible to hold on through external shaking. Instead, you must keep shaking your own snow globe and disrupting yourself and your leadership. Otherwise, you'll be a victim to all of the external disruption and shaking.

You must also remember that external disruption is not the same as internal disruption. Many leaders, teams and organizations believe that they've been shaking and shifting through the pandemic, but many of them are merely reacting to the external disruptions. The biggest difference between external disruptions and internal shifts is intention and commitment. When you react to a situation, it's just that—a reaction—but disruptive shifts are what happen when we do our own shaking and shifting, and then follow through with the disruptive shifts in thinking, perspectives, actions and leadership.

My final thought on regular snow globe and leadership shaking is this: *if you don't regularly shake your own snow globe, other people, situations and even life itself will shake it for you.* That's the thing about snow globes—they're meant to be shaken, and your life is just the same. If you don't shake your own snow globe, you'll experience life as being out of control (as if someone or something else is shaking things up), and that's true. When you fail to shake things up on your own, then situations, experiences and people will create a shaken-up experience for you because you've given up control of your snow globe. In other words, you've become a victim of shaking rather than the victor of your own leadership and life shaking experiences.

The first step is to shake your personal leadership and life snow globe, and don't stop with one or just an occasional shaking. Once you shake your snow globe, keep shaking it regularly and pay close attention to what you see when your shaking creates a new and usually different perspective on whatever situation, challenge or opportunity is in front of you.

If you're ready to re-empower yourself, to reclaim responsibility for your life, your impact and your outcomes, and to experience your leadership, life and relationships in different and deeper ways, then it's time to shake your snow globe. Not only now, but regularly because all perspective and outcome shifts start when you're willing to shake things up starting with yourself.

# Chapter 2

# The Leadership Gap

WHERE HAVE ALL the leaders gone? That's a question that tens of millions of people and team members have been asking for some time, and the questions have been amplified during the COVID pandemic. When the time comes that we can say with some confidence that we're past the pandemic, people will be saying one of these two things about their positional or empowered leaders:

Thank you for being there for me!

or

Where were you when I needed you?

Notably, this is not a new situation or reality since people have been feeling this way about their leaders and leadership for many years.

In fact, as I've spoken to audiences about leadership for the past dozen plus years I often give them this assignment: Write down the great leaders you know and interact with. You can probably guess how long this assignment takes—just a moment or two since most of us don't know many great leaders. We may know some good managers or operators. We know some "successful" business owners and leaders, but that's sadly different from great leadership. Part of the problem is that we're unclear on what exactly makes a great leader.

## THE STATE OF LEADERSHIP

If you're wondering about the state of leadership, the best place to look is at the state of engagement. Employee engagement guru Gallup has been studying teams and team engagement since 2000, and here's what they've discovered as of 2019:[1]

* Active engagement was at an all-time "high" of thirty-five percent (35%)
* Actively disengaged team members were at an all-time low of thirteen percent (13%)
* Not engaged team members were at an all-time low of fifty-two percent (52%)

Really, an all-time low of "only" 52% of team members NOT engaged?

For comparison, in 2000 the percentages were: Engaged (26%), Actively Disengaged (18%) and Not Engaged (56%).[2] Certainly, an improvement over the past twenty years but nothing to brag about. But then came COVID—active engagement ranged from a new high of thirty-nine percent (39%) in January 2021 to a low of thirty-one percent (31%) in June 2020.

While there has been some improvement with feedback and hybrid employee engagement, Gallup reports the following as of February 2021:[3] 1. Those who work from home all or nearly all of the time reported higher burnout; 2. Engaged workers are at risk if wellbeing is low; 3. Manager engagement is too low. In short, we have some work to do on team engagement and this is a matter of leadership.

One more key and recent Gallup finding is that most organizations are "failing" at developing their managers as leaders.[4] This included the following findings:

- Seventy percent (70%) of a team's engagement is influenced by managers
- The expectation is for the manager to be more of a coach than a boss
- Most companies' records on manager development are "dismal"

Thus, the opening of this chapter—where have all the leaders gone?

## THE MISSION OF LEADERSHIP

A big part of the trouble with leadership is we've lost sight of the singular focus of leadership. We've also gotten locked into the positional leadership mindset—the idea that leadership is based upon titles, positions and rank. Let's first get clear on what is THE focus of leadership—it's people. Leaders lead people. Leaders impact people. Leaders support and encourage people. Leaders help grow people and accomplish outcomes with people, not through people. Sadly, this is not the norm today as many leaders have fallen into "leading" projects, organizations and initiatives, often forgetting that leadership is about the people.

In addition, today many people are promoted into leadership positions based upon being high performing doers, but once they're in positions of leadership they're being judged based upon their people skills and character. Thus, they're "successful" and rewarded for being great doers but then they're promoted into leadership roles and expected to do even more *and* lead more. See the problem?

My singular premise for leaders is that they have a single mission— to support, develop and grow their people. After all, we don't lead projects—we lead the people who hopefully are empowered to execute

*Leadership is about everything that touches and impacts people.*

the project (versus being directed to complete tasks as part of the project). Within this mission is the objective of creating a safe place for growth, collaboration, execution and impact. My simple litmus test is that leadership is about everything that touches and impacts people, with a goal toward building authentic followership (more on this later in the book).

Let's now address our attachment to positional leadership. Simon Sinek famously offered, "Leadership is not a rank or a position, it is a choice—a choice to look after the person to the left of us and the person to the right of us." The idea that leadership is strictly organizational and based upon rank, position, title or anointment has caused us to forget that leadership is everywhere, that everyone has the opportunity to lead and that leadership is about moments. If I ask team members who their leader is they'll almost always name the people with leadership titles or positions. However, when I instead ask them who demonstrates the strongest leadership qualities, they often refer to someone on their team that has a limited or no title or position. This is the reality of leadership—everyone has the opportunity to lead when leadership moments arise and it's a choice each of us can make in that moment (choosing to lead or not to lead).

When I speak about leadership and leadership development, I encourage everyone to embrace their leadership opportunities and to remember that you can lead wherever you are. One of my favorite movies is the HBO series *Band of Brothers* focusing on a company of paratroopers during World War II, but it's really a story about great leadership and terrible leadership. People leadership versus positional leadership. Trust-based leadership versus command and control leadership. Influence leadership versus power driven leadership. While the main character (Major Dick Winters) is the focus of the leadership story and certainly one worth studying and emulating, there's a small scene that's worthy of checking out when it comes to understanding that leadership is not positional. Captain Speirs is telling First Sergeant Lipton that his platoon has had a good leader for some time:

Speirs:  "I've been told there's always been one man they could count on. … Every day kept the spirits up, kept the men focused and gave them direction. All the things a good combat leader does. You don't have any idea who I'm talking about do you?"

Lipton:  "No sir."

Speirs:  "Hell, it was you first sergeant. Ever since Winters made battalion you've been the leader of Easy Company."

Check out the video clip here: https://youtu.be/3JhIFd-iKz8. This is a powerful reminder that leadership is not bestowed … it's claimed, lived and put into action. Notice the key phrase above—"one man they could count on"—this is the essence of leadership.

## Leadership Moments

The reality of business and life is that each of us has opportunities to lead every day, whether it be with our business, our job, our team, our families, our relationships, our communities and even ourselves. It also becomes crystal clear that leadership is not a 24 / 7 "job" because even positional leaders spend only a small percentage of their time leading. Most of us spend the majority of our time taking care of tasks, getting work done or producing in some way, none of which is leadership (other than leadership by example). What leadership does involve and require is 24 / 7 awareness—to always be scanning, anticipating and stepping into the leadership moments and opportunities.

Let's look at one typical example that occurs nearly every day in business. Let's face it, we generally don't do meetings well, and I rarely hear team members saying that their meetings are effective and that they wish they had more meetings. There are many issues with meetings but one big one is the many times and ways that we get off course in a meeting (what I call going down a rabbit trail that's off-agenda, not a priority and a distraction for nearly everyone). What typically happens in these situations is that everyone in the room is looking to the supposed leader (whoever called the meeting) to make the course correction, but the truth is that everyone in the room has the leadership opportunity to step out, speak up and get the meeting back on course.

However, there are obstacles and fears to stepping in. What will the supposed leader think? Will they think I'm stepping on their toes? What will the people down the rabbit trail think of me? Is this my job? What will everyone else think if I speak up? And yet what's required in this moment is leadership—someone willing to take the risk of speaking up to do what's best and right for the meeting, the team and the objectives. Of course, there are risks including those listed above, but taking risks is the essence of leadership. That's why I call this opportunity *stepping into the fires of leadership*, because it's hot and risky. That's how we know this is a leadership moment—it involves people, communication and taking action at the risk of impacting people. It's also an opportunity to do what you believe is best for the moment, team and organization, including modeling for others what it means to lead in the moments.

## LEADERSHIP TODAY

Today's business reality is that five (5) leadership traits are topping every list as vital for effective and impactful leadership:

1. Vulnerability
2. Authenticity
3. Empathy
4. Self-Awareness
5. Emotional Intelligence

In other words, bringing more humanity to leadership and leading in a way that recognizes and honors that our people are human beings.

During a podcast interview on our Leadership Junkies Podcast (www.leadershipjunkies.com), President and Co-Founder Larry English (Centric Consulting) was asked what the secret sauce was for building a culture of trust, high team engagement and a caring team. Larry's response was illuminating:[5]

❋ Model and teach vulnerability ("a shortcut to trust")

❋ Invite your people to bring their whole self to work

*To lead is to be human.*

Similarly, countless thought leaders (including this author) believe that vulnerability is critical in leadership (e.g., Simon Sinek, Walt Rakowich, Brene Brown). Virtually every guest on Leadership Junkies Podcast has listed vulnerability as a key leadership foundation, including guest Lee Chambers who offered that "...to lead is to be human."[6] As Simon Sinek said, "The great leaders are not the strongest, they are the ones who are honest about their weaknesses."

## What's the Gap?

Despite this overwhelming consensus of what leadership is required today (from experts, thought leaders and team members), there's an enormous leadership gap in organizations, families, communities and governments. This book is designed to close that gap and to offer you tangible and actionable shifts in your leadership so you can be the leader you choose to be in every part of your business and life.

In my leadership journey and in talking to thousands of leaders (and potential followers) I've discerned three (3) specific reasons for the leadership gap:

1. Fears
2. Inconsistent Modeling
3. Blind Spots

In *Transfluence: How to Lead with Transformative Influence in Today's Climates of Change* (Post Hill Press 2020), Walt Rakowich cites a 2014 survey by Roger Jones of Vantage Hill Partners in London which found these five buckets of the biggest fears of leaders:

1. Incompetence
2. Underachieving
3. Appearing too vulnerable
4. Being attacked politically by colleagues
5. Looking foolish

*Transfluence* at page 62. The problem—these top fears are in direct conflict with a leader demonstrating vulnerability in her or his leadership.

I was born in 1959 and began my working career in 1984, and I know that leadership for my generation and my father's generation was all about command and control—do what you're told and do it well. There was also little attention given to or concern for team engagement. In fact, the typical leadership mindset in the late 20th Century was that a paycheck should be sufficient to engage your team (and it usually was). In addition, team members were generally not thinking about how engaged, happy or safe they were at work—it was all about working hard and performing well. Thus, many people who are in leadership positions today are simply leading the way they were led (e.g. praise means not getting criticized, the only feedback is critical and you should be happy to have a job).

In extreme contrast, today's employees want to be engaged, want to be developed, want to feel safe (physically, mentally and emotionally) and want to be connected with a mission. However, many current leaders weren't led this way, were never shown this type of leadership (in fact, it wasn't even discussed) and were successful because they worked hard, didn't ask questions and were high performers. In essence, today's leaders are being encouraged to lead in ways they've never seen or experienced, and without ever being trained or developed in this form of vulnerable, authentic and people-focused leadership. No wonder we have a leadership gap.

Finally, blind spots are a leadership reality including when it comes to the ways that leaders see themselves as leaders. As leadership speaker and author Tommy Spaulding (best-selling author of *It's Not Just Who You Know* and *The Heart-Led Leader*) shared on Leadership Junkies Podcast:[7]

* ❅ "There's a choice that every leader has to make. Serve others before yourself and be a servant leader or be a self-serving leader and serve yourself first."

* ❅ "In twenty years of this business I've never had anybody ever say to me you know Tommy, 'I'm a self-serving leader,' so basically 90% of people call themselves servant leaders yet only 10% really are."

Adding to this, Tommy shared that leaders don't get to decide if they're a self-serving leader or a servant leader ... the people around you decide. "Your wife, your husband, your children, your employees, your customers, your clients, your friends, your neighbors. They decide."[8] "When you interview their people it's usually a huge disconnect. ... Most self-serving leaders don't even know that they're self-serving leaders."[9]

In other words, most leaders already believe they're leading with vulnerability, authenticity, empathy, self-awareness and emotional intelligence. So how do you transform your leadership when you think you're already there? This is the biggest blind spot in leadership.

One other obstacle is a matter of mindset and language. One of the most disempowering and debilitating phrases in leadership today is "soft skills" (as opposed to hard or technical skills). The simplest definition of soft skills is people skills and skills that relate to communication, relationships and collaboration. You'd think these skills would get a great deal of attention and investment (of time, energy and dollars), but the opposite is often true. Imagine sitting in a meeting asking a question about where to invest in the coming year—hard / technical skills or soft skills. Unfortunately, we often perceive hard skills as delivering more easily measurable results, and thus we shift our attention and dollars in that direction.

The truth is that when it comes to leadership (which is about people), soft skills and people skills are the most important and impactful. That's why I refer to "soft" skills as *impact skills*. The other value of soft skills is that the return on soft skills is exponential and a multiplier, while the return on hard skills is linear ($1 + 1 = 2$). In addition, growth in soft skills has a ripple effect while hard skills typically only create a singular impact. While this may seem like a matter of semantics, the words we use often determine how we see something (e.g. growth and development). You've likely heard the saying that "no one ever got fired for buying IBM," and the same goes for training and development—no one ever got fired for doing hard skills training.

The truth of leadership and growth is that soft skills development is the secret sauce for enhancing communication, relationships, innovation, team engagement, team growth, trust, accountability and impact. If you only want your team to be more efficient, then investing in hard / technical skills might achieve your objective. However, if you want to grow your leadership, culture, team, impact and outcomes, then soft skills development demands your time, attention and resources.

I'll talk more about each of these in the coming chapters, but for now, assess yourself in what ways your leadership is being impacted or held back by any of these blind spots and obstacles.

# A Formula for Heartful Leadership

Before we continue this leadership journey, I want to share a formula with you … one that you can use to better understand your own leadership and the path to being a leader of authentic influence and followership.

As you'll see, the starting point is that the end game is about impact, not outcomes, because leaders know that outcomes are part of and flow from the impact we create with and through our leadership.

- Impact flows from influence
- Influence flows from trust
- Trust flows from authentic and empathetic listening
- Listening flows from caring
- Caring flows from the heart

In other words, to create more impact with and through your leadership (wherever you're leading), you start with the heart which leads you down the path to impact. Most importantly, imagine how people around you (including teams) would experience you, your leadership and your culture if you led with this mindset and approach?

The rest of this book is designed to deliver to you mindset shifts, awarenesses and tangible tools to help you lead this way. And if you're bold enough, courageous enough and vulnerable enough to open yourself up to this different way of leading, you WILL build trust, build relationships, grow people, grow followership and create an environment where people feel safe, seen and valued. This is the secret sauce of leadership, engagement and impact today!

# Chapter 3

# The Trouble with Trust

GET READY TO dive into the deep end of the leadership pool because we're headed where we must always begin in business, life and relationships—with trust—the foundation of it all. Despite being such a critical element of leadership, trust is a topic that often gets the least amount of direct attention (if any at all) for many reasons. In fact, it's rarely discussed individually, in organizations or as a team. And it's time to bring trust into the light of leadership where it belongs.

Let's start with big three challenges when it comes to trust:

1. We don't understand how it can be disruptive
2. Therefore, we don't want to talk about it (because it's terrifying)
3. So, we assume trust is there and rarely work on it

The short and critical point is this: ALL business issues boil down to trust issues!

**Why don't we understand it?** It's simple—because trust is complex, multi-faceted and contextual. Let's start with a scenario:

> Think about the person you trust most and now picture that person in your mind. Now answer this question: *Would you trust that person to perform complex surgery on someone you care about?*

Unless this person is a surgeon skilled in the type of surgery that's needed, your answer is "no", and yet this is the person you trust most. This is just a glimpse of all the complexities of trust.

Here's a list of just some of the contextual elements of trust or lack of trust:

* Trust of intent—What do you believe about a person's intentions?

* Trust of caring—Do you believe the person cares about you or not?

* Trust of skills—What level of skills does the person have that are relevant to the task?

* Trust of experience—What prior experience does this person have relative to what's needed?

* Trust of industry—Is this person in a high trust industry (e.g. nurses) or a low trust industry (e.g. car sales)?

* Trust of position—What beliefs and biases do you have about the positions that people hold (e.g. C-suite, management, middle management, administrative, factory)?

* Trust of differences (one of our natural biases is to trust people that are most like us)—What biases (often unconscious) do you have about people who are in any way different from you?

* Trust of consistency—How consistent is a person with their behavior (e.g. their actions seem consistent, yet trust has not been built)?

❋ Trust of alignment—Do the person's actions align with their words and stated beliefs or values, and if not, what's the impact on your trust levels?

We could do a deep dive into each of these but for now it's enough to understand that trust is impacted by so many different factors, many of which we'll be discussing in this chapter and throughout the book.

Before we move to the next facet, keep in mind that all of the foregoing, and our overall trust levels of a person, a team or an organization, are greatly impacted and informed by our prior history and experiences (what I call trust baggage). The key point is to assume and expect that every person on your team has some form of trust baggage, rather than assuming they're a blank slate, which is what many leaders do to their detriment.

**Why We Don't Want to Talk About It**. Just as simply as above, it's because it's uncomfortable and potentially the most terrifying conversation we can have. Imagine looking someone in the eyes and telling them you don't trust them—generally, or with respect to a certain issue, task, project, etc. Before we dive more into what terrifies us about trust, let's address the fact that trust is not sexy.

A few years ago, I discovered a truth about trust and culture that shocked but didn't surprise me. Most of you are familiar with *Fortune's* annual recognition of the 100 Best Companies to Work For, which typically is littered with well-known companies and brands. Notably, *Fortune* lists key elements of what makes each company a great place to work—all the cool, sexy, and unique things that make them the best companies to work for. These "sexy" elements include things like cool offices, enhanced benefits, unique compensation systems, flexible work schedules, etc. In many cases, the attributes of the "best companies" are not easily accessible to small and mid-sized companies, but it turns out there was an obfuscated twist (at least until 2012).

Prior to 2012, there was a footnote tucked away in the back of *Fortune* that said the following: "Two-thirds of a company's score is based on the results of the Great Place To Work's Trust Index Survey." Today, this fact is openly shared and known to all, but why was this critical fact—trust not only matters but it's the most important factor—hidden away in a footnote? Simple: because it's not sexy and perhaps trust doesn't sell magazines. Why isn't this fact—that trust is the key to great companies, cultures and workplaces—shouted from the mountain tops? Back to the opening answer—because trust isn't sexy and it's a terrifying topic.

Let's unpack the terrifying part. A good friend recently shared this with me. He was talking to his wife about something, sensed some uncertainty, and asked her this question: "Do you trust me to handle this?" Her answer: "No." Wow. He admitted it was difficult to hear, but vital for her to share if they were to get to the heart of the issue. Otherwise, we're trying to address communication, process or execution issues, when the actual issue is trust. Thankfully, their relationship is based upon trust, which allowed them to have the "trust" conversation even if it was uncomfortable.

Based upon my own experiences over the years, I've become a fan of and believe in the importance of having direct trust conversations. Early in my business, I was working with a small business of approximately 30 team members. They were experiencing a challenge with one person. This team member had recently had her first baby and despite exemplary quality of work, she was habitually late to work. While there had been efforts to accommodate her situation, there was still a need for her to be timely in her work arrival and start time. In fact, it had gotten to the point where they were considering terminating her and they were looking for solutions.

My suggestion was to conduct a 360-degree review process for the entire team. Yes, everyone. I encouraged them to be honest because it would best serve each team member, the team overall and the organization. Through this process, the team member my colleagues were struggling with was reviewed by the entire team. Not only did she score low on timeliness, but she also scored low on reliability and nearly half of the team members wrote a note that said some version of "I can't count on her." She was devastated by this feedback and was highly emotional when hearing it. However, this was the honest feedback that she needed to hear to change her behavior. The problem is she had previously seen her tardiness as isolated behavior and all the encouragement to be on time had missed the mark. However, when she realized that the impact of her tardiness was that her fellow team members couldn't rely on her (a trust issue), she got it. While she continued to have struggles with her schedule, she quickly transformed her behavior and was largely consistent in being on time.

The reality is, we don't always see or address trust issues. I once was introduced to the CEO of a large, third generation family business (over 1,000 employees and hundreds of millions in revenue). Their senior human resources leader was concerned their business was losing its values and culture. Shortly before our lunch, the senior leadership team (16 colleagues who reported to the CEO) had been surveyed and one of the key discoveries was a general consensus that the senior leaders believed that the CEO didn't trust them. When I asked the CEO about these survey results, he said they didn't make sense and that his team was "wrong." According to the CEO, "it's not that I don't trust them—I just don't feel like I can count on them." Excuse me, isn't that precisely what trust means? Yet, this CEO chose not to accept his team's input regarding how they didn't feel that he trusted them and instead labeled it differently. Again, a lack of trust is a terrifying concept, and our avoidance of the conversation and issue is to our great peril.

A few years ago, I was speaking to a group of global business owners, and I shared thoughts and perspectives on the importance, role and challenges of trust. My conclusion was that the willingness to have the trust conversation with team members—clarifying that the issue is a lack of trust and being as specific as possible about the lack of trust—will transform their leadership, culture, team and performance. A week later, I received an email from one of the attendees who shared that they'd had the "trust conversation" with one of their team members who was struggling in their performance and not responding to improvement guidance. The leader acknowledged how fearful he'd been of having the conversation and that it was difficult to start, but he indicated that the team member (although difficult to hear) had seemed to hear it and "get it." While it was early in the process, they were, for the first time, seeing dramatic shifts in the team member's performance and they were now optimistic of a favorable outcome for the team member and the organization.

This is why trust is such a disruptive and challenging issue in any organization and is why it's up to you as a leader to be bold and courageous in shaking up your conversations and solutions. This is simply the nature of leadership. You'll likely have team members who are not open to or ready to have the trust conversation and you'll have to discern what to do next. Is their reluctance a function of their past experiences with you as the leader? Are there prior trust issues with the team or organization? Or is it their own unwillingness to take responsibility for the lack of trust that they've engendered? This discernment will determine what comes next with the team members. If they're unwilling to have the trust conversations and / or address the ways that they've created or contributed to the lack of trust, they may need to depart the organization.

*Trust is a complex concept.*

**Why do we assume trust?** Because of all the reasons listed above. We like to believe that we're trustworthy and we want to avoid any form of the trust conversation. We also forget that trust is a complex concept. Frankly, who wants to admit that they or their organization have trust issues? But trust issues are everywhere and they're often dressed up as other issues such as:

- ❄ Communication issues
- ❄ Feedback issues
- ❄ Process issues
- ❄ Meeting issues
- ❄ Performance issues
- ❄ Execution issues
- ❄ Culture issues
- ❄ Burnout issues
- ❄ Quality issues
- ❄ Safety issues
- ❄ Engagement issues
- ❄ Elephant issues (the elephants that show up in the room)

I think you get the point. What I've discovered is, whatever issues or challenges an organization, team or leader are dealing with, there are underlying trust issues. The problem is if you don't address the trust issues, any solution will be half-baked and the trust issues will continue to surface. It's kind of like painting over a rusted surface without sanding out the rust, filling it in and first painting it with a primer. It may look good for a short time but eventually the rust will come through in full force. Trust is the same way.

## WHY TRUST MATTERS

While I'd love to believe that the importance of trust is obvious, the lack of attention we give it makes it vital to share with you the key reasons that trust matters. Here's the short list:

- Trust is the foundation of followership (people only voluntarily follow people they trust)
- Trust is an accelerator for getting things done
- Trust is essential for innovation and creativity
- Trust is vital for people to take risks (versus always hesitating)
- Trust is required for people to be willing to challenge the status quo
- Trust is the linchpin for teamwork
- Trust is the foundation for a culture of safety (see Chapter 5)
- Trust is the essence of engagement
- Trust is the facilitator of high performance
- Trust is the key ingredient for workplace fun and joy
- Trust is the lifeblood of relationships

A recent Harvard Business Review article highlighted, "Compared with people at low-trust companies, people at high-trust companies report: 74% less stress, 106% more energy at work, 50% higher productivity, 13% fewer sick days, 76% more engagement, 29% more satisfaction with their lives, 40% less burnout."[10] Not a bad return on trust!

Is that all, you say?

Let's face a couple of simple truths:

❋ People ONLY voluntarily follow people they trust

❋ If people don't feel trusted or don't trust the people they work with, they withhold everything you desire from your people, including:

  ❋ Ideas

  ❋ Support

  ❋ Encouragement

  ❋ Feedback

  ❋ Questions

  ❋ Care and concern

  ❋ Commitment

  ❋ Selflessness (versus selfishness)

  ❋ Accountability and responsibility

  ❋ "We" (versus "me")

  ❋ Engagement

❋ Trust is easily broken, slowly rebuilt and likely impacted by everything we do and say (and don't do and don't say)

In short, trust is the secret sauce of leadership, teams, culture, relationships and performance. Therefore, it's time to explore the ways we build, nurture and break trust.

## TRUST FOUNDATIONS

As a starting point for trust, we need to consider the three basic mindsets that every person might have with respect to trust, all of which are based upon prior trust experiences:

1. Natural Trust—Someone who typically trusts people they interact with unless and until they're given reasons to take back or withhold trust.

2. Neutral Trust—Someone who neither trusts nor distrusts people they interact with and makes their trust discernments based upon their experiences with that person.

3. Natural Distrust—Someone who typically distrusts people they interact with and withholds trust unless and until they're given sufficient proof of trust to begin to trust.

I'm not going to suggest that any of these three is the "right" or "best" mindset, however, be aware that despite the potential pros and cons of each, building trust-based relationships is the most difficult for those who naturally distrust. The reason is simple—these are people who only trust if someone first overcomes their distrust and then builds upon it to get to some level of trust. The natural distruster will also likely expect or desire that they be trusted while withholding their trust of others. See the issues?

One thing to consider is that your typical starting mindset for trust is almost certainly based upon prior trust or broken trust experiences. Therefore, exploring the source of your trust mindset and processing those sources may allow you to make small or large shifts. Think of it this way—it's extremely difficult to trust someone who doesn't trust you, so our foundational trust mindsets play an important role in who we trust *and* who trusts you.

## TRUST BUILDERS AND BREAKERS

I regularly work with organizations and teams and we always have conversations about trust. Over the years, I've done hundreds of workshops where trust is one of the core topics and I've developed a simple process to open the trust discussions. I put everyone into small groups and ask them to answer these two questions:

1. What are the key ways to build trust?
2. What are the key ways to break trust?

I then give them time to make their lists and then get everyone back together in the larger group. Without telling them ahead of time, I then ask people to stand up if they started with the list of ways to break trust first. Typically, 90% of the people stand up. Why? The breaking trust list is easier to itemize because there are many ways to break trust and we see it being broken every day. The trust building list is usually very short and NEVER lists more than six ways.

Here's some of the typical things listed on the breaking trust list:

* Don't do what you say you're going to do
* Say one thing and do another (don't walk your talk)
* Be late to meetings (especially your own) or be late in completing things
* Lie / cheat
* Talk about other people behind their back (gossip)
* Don't have peoples' backs
* Take excess credit (fail to give or share credit)
* Blame other people / teams
* Poor listening (talk too much)
* Engage in verbal abuse of others
* Talk down to others
* Act like you're better than other people
* Unleash anger on others
* Ass-kissing
* Posing
* Inappropriate / insensitive humor
* Demonstrate favoritism
* Bullshitter (hype or oversell yourself)
* Hijack conversations to talk about yourself
* Unfair or unequal standards or expectations
* Self-centered behavior

Of course, we could go on and on. The issue is we often don't consciously equate many of the preceding points as trust breakers but rather as things that cause us not to like someone (also true). The key is to realize the many, many ways that we break trust every day and almost always without intending to do so.

Now, let's look at the much shorter trust builders list:

1.  Don't do the things on the trust breakers list (this is nearly always listed as No. 1 on the trust builders list)

2.  Do what you say you're going to do and take responsibility when you don't (self-accountability)

3.  Align your actions with your words, beliefs and stated values (integrity)

4.  Demonstrate genuine care and concern for others through your actions (empathy)

5.  Model vulnerability (see Chapter 4)[11]

6.  Make time for people and be present (presence)

We'll be diving into all of these trust builders throughout this book. For now, the key takeaway is that leadership requires that we intentionally and actively engage in building trust and be even more intentional and committed to minimizing the trust breakers.

If you're thinking that we should avoid the trust breakers entirely, then you've hit your first big blind spot. We all mess up when it comes to trust, but one of the biggest misses is not realizing that whatever our behavior was, it diminished trust. This refers back to our tendency of assuming things as it relates to trust—we assume our screw ups and mistakes are just that and without any trust impact. This is especially true when we play the apology card and other people say, "It's okay. Don't worry about it." Apologies (even when accepted) don't necessarily correct the breaks in trust or even minimize them. In fact, in some cases the apologies further diminish trust especially if people don't see changes in behavior.

This is why one of my strong statements about leadership (prepare yourself) is that leaders shouldn't apologize. Instead, they actually should change. This doesn't mean that you shouldn't apologize for your choices, actions and impacts, but it does mean that people don't trust apologies—they trust commitment to and demonstrated change in behavior. While some people are initially shocked when I say "leaders don't apologize," they quickly get it when I ask them, "How many of you are tired of people apologizing and continuing to do the same thing again, only to apologize again?" Just keep this in mind when it comes to trust: your people are all from Missouri (the Show Me state) and they want you to show them who you are (not tell them who you are). They want you to show them that you're trustworthy, not only tell them you're trustworthy.

And if you think being in a leadership position earns you trust, you've found another blind spot. People in leadership positions are often accorded a degree of respect due to their position, but everything else (and especially trust) is earned by consistently engaging in trust building behaviors, minimizing your trust breaking actions and immediately taking full responsibility for your actions and impact when you mess up.

## Trust Me

As we wrap up this critical conversation about trust and leadership, I encourage you to leave this chapter with these five truths top in mind:

1. Trust is THE foundation of leadership.
2. Building trust requires intentionality, commitment and consistent action.
3. Trust breaking action is inevitable and must be met with full and immediate responsibility for actions and impact.
4. Trust conversations can be intimidating, yet it's vital that they happen (and the more trust in your organization, the easier these conversations are).
5. Every issue you have has a trust issue at the core.

# Chapter 4

# Time to Get Naked

"What?" you say?

"Naked?"

Yes it's a play on words because this chapter is about a foundational element of present-day impactful leadership. *Naked* is the perfect word because this critical foundation is vulnerability, the most terrifying and misunderstood concept in business and leadership today. In fact, it's so challenging that this chapter may make you uncomfortable and that's a form of vulnerability—the willingness to be uncomfortable and still hang in there.

Before going further, let's just get real and acknowledge that vulnerability in leadership is not only uncomfortable but disruptive in that it's not been the way most of you were led, and you've likely not had vulnerable leadership modeled for you by others. In fact, embracing vulnerability as a foundation of your leadership will likely require the most shaking and shifting of any of the concepts in this book. As a result, your willingness to shake up your leadership in the direction of vulnerability will also pay the biggest returns in impact, trust and influence. As I've said so many times, great discomfort always precedes great outcomes and this is certainly true when it comes to choosing to be a vulnerable leader.

As we highlighted in Chapter 2, the Big V (vulnerability) is at the forefront of leadership and business discussions today. As Larry English emphasized in a podcast interview with the Leadership Junkies, the secret sauce for building a culture of trust in an organization is modeling vulnerability from the top-down.[12] Larry also referred to vulnerability as "a shortcut to trust" (see Chapter 3 on trust). The verdict from thought leaders around the world—Tommy Spaulding, Simon Sinek, Walt Rakowich, Brene Brown, etc.—is that vulnerability is critical in leadership. Remarkably, vulnerability itself was rarely the topic of conversation in the business world. That is, until Brene Brown brought it center stage via two of her compelling TED Talks in 2010 and 2012:

❋ The Power of Vulnerability (over 52 million views as of May 2021 … No. 4 all time)[13]
❋ Listening to Shame (nearly 16 million views as of May 2021)[14]

Brene Brown (an academic researcher) shared that vulnerability is the linchpin of relationships, connection, joy and creativity. Notably, after her 2010 TED Talk, Brene was a highly sought after speaker for businesses and business audiences, but as Brene shares in her 2012 TED Talk, business leaders wanted her to avoid two topics—vulnerability and shame:

> "One of the weird things that's happened is, after the TED explosion, I got a lot of offers to speak all over the country— everyone from schools and parent meetings to Fortune 500 companies. And so many of the calls went like this, 'Dr. Brown, we loved your TED talk. We'd like you to come in and speak. We'd appreciate it if you wouldn't mention vulnerability or shame.'"[15]

What? Don't mention vulnerability and shame—the very core of her message? Thus, we see the challenge that continues today—deep resistance to being vulnerable and not allowing vulnerability to even become part of the conversation. And while the resistance is real and strong, leaders must move past and through the discomfort and fear to show their own vulnerability. By doing so, leaders create a safe environment for their team to also be vulnerable.

Before we continue stripping down vulnerability to its naked truth, let's explore a reality that we must acknowledge to better understand vulnerability. Here's the truth that seems to be eluding us—*vulnerability requires vulnerability*.

"What?" you say? "That makes no sense, Jeff. It's a circular position."

But it's not. What it means is the *external* vulnerability we model, demonstrate and show to others requires *internal* vulnerability.

Vulnerability is about taking risks—primarily risks of judgment from others. Unless and until you're willing to take those internal risks of vulnerability, you'll never be able to demonstrate outward vulnerability. And let's face it—our default is to avoid or minimize risks, especially risks to ourselves. As a result, it's vital that we become more aware of our instincts to protect ourselves. By taking more personal risks, the people around us are able to experience our *external vulnerability* as we more consciously practice our *internal* vulnerability.

If you're wondering why we struggle so mightily with vulnerability, it's because we're talking about leading in a way that's still largely uncharted territory. Even the English language is set up to discourage us from embracing vulnerability. Specifically, there's no word that matches being vulnerable in leadership, nor is there a word for vulnerability in leadership.

There are definitions but they're not encouraging.

* ✳ Vulnerable: "able to be easily physically, emotionally, or mentally hurt, influenced or attacked." (Cambridge Dictionary)
* ✸ Vulnerability: "the quality of being vulnerable (able to be easily hurt, influenced, or attacked) or something that is vulnerable." (Cambridge Dictionary)
* ✸ Vulnerable: "1: capable of being physically or emotionally wounded. 2: open to attack or damage." (Merriam-Webster Dictionary)

Even when one dictionary (Dictionary.com) includes a definition in the context of communication, relationships and leadership, it's not very encouraging: "willingness to show emotion or to allow one's **weakness** to be seen or known; willingness to risk being hurt or attacked (emphasis added)."

Not only do our dictionary definitions not encourage vulnerability as a practice, but they set up vulnerability as something terrifying and to be avoided at all costs. No wonder we struggle with it!

And yet, we all know the relationship and trust-building power of vulnerability *IF* we're willing to take the risk to be vulnerable. This is why Brene Brown's wisdom on vulnerability is so impactful:

> "There's two things that I've learned in the last year. The first is vulnerability is not weakness. And that myth is profoundly dangerous. […] How many of you think of vulnerability and weakness synonymously? The majority of people do. Now let me ask you this question: This past week at TED, how many of you, when you saw vulnerability up here, thought it was pure courage? Vulnerability is not weakness. I define vulnerability as emotional risk, exposure, uncertainty. It fuels our daily lives. And I've come to the belief [t]hat vulnerability is our most accurate measurement of courage—to be vulnerable, to let ourselves be seen, to be honest."[16]

Indeed, being vulnerable and leading with vulnerability inevitably involves taking personal risks, which is why your willingness to model external vulnerability is the "most accurate measurement of courage." I'm hoping you're easily grasping the important role of vulnerability in leadership, yet it's still a disruptive concept because of so many decades of an absence of vulnerability in leadership. This is why committing to vulnerability in your leadership requires so much internal disruption and snow globe shaking.

*Vulnerability is the golden ticket to leadership.*

I'd simplify and clarify the connection between leadership and vulnerability this way: *Vulnerability in leadership is consciously taking the risk of exposing your humanness.* People follow who they trust—

and they only trust people who they authentically know and fully experience. Vulnerability is the path to allowing people to know and experience you. Thus, vulnerability is the golden ticket to leadership and influence essentials, especially trust.

Author and leadership thought leader Walt Rakowich has this to say about the role of trust in leadership:

> "[T]he one thing that I learned is the importance of trust. You know, with trust as a leader, you have everything. Without trust you have nothing, absolutely nothing."[17]

So it's clear that impactful and influential leadership cannot exist or succeed without vulnerability and the trust that it seeds and feeds. In case you're asking yourself, "but what about command and control, dictatorial and fear-based leadership? Do they require vulnerability?" Of course not, and best of luck with trying to "lead" that way in the 21st Century!

## TAKING THE EMOTION OUT OF VULNERABILITY

Yes, you read that correctly. We need to take the emotion out of vulnerability. Well, not fully but mostly, because in leadership one of the biggest obstacles to vulnerability is the misconception of always aligning emotions with vulnerability. In fact, we often amp up our resistance to vulnerability by attaching so much "emotion" to it.

Many years ago, I was coaching a business owner and her team, and she shared with me that the prior year had been extremely difficult as she had nursed her ailing father until he passed just a few months earlier. She admitted that it had been a very challenging year and that it had taken a high emotional toll on her. When I asked her how much her team had seen and experienced of her challenging year, she quickly responded: "Virtually nothing. I couldn't bring that here [to work]." When I inquired further about it, she said "What did you expect me to do? Lay on the floor weeping, which is what I do at home?" Notice how she took my question and immediately invoked a situation that, of course, was not what I was suggesting. In other words, she created a version of emotional vulnerability that didn't make sense, and thus, a reason to avoid vulnerability.

I hung in with her during the conversation and followed up by asking her this question: "What might your team conclude about you as a person and leader when you showed virtually no emotion while your father was dying and ultimately died?" In response, her shoulders slumped a bit and she said, "Hmmm, that I'm cold hearted and didn't love my father." Exactly! While vulnerability carries a risk (that's just the deal), the absence or withholding of vulnerability also carries a risk—a risk that's even more likely to occur than the potential risks of modeling vulnerability.

Let's be clear about emotions and vulnerability—being vulnerable doesn't mean being emotional, but it may mean showing emotions when those feelings are authentic. In other words, allow yourself to be human and to demonstrate that humanity by allowing your emotions to be witnessed by others. This is one example of what it means to be naked as a leader—to be human. When people ask me if being vulnerable means crying in front of people, I ask them, "Well, do you feel like crying?" If so, then vulnerability likely means allowing the tears to be seen and experienced. Vulnerability is not about acting or showing something that's not real, but it is about showing whatever is real. And the fundamental reason is simple—vulnerability is the gateway to connection and connection is the gateway to relationships. *AND* leadership is a relationship enterprise.

> *Leadership is a relationship enterprise.*

## THE TRUTH ABOUT VULNERABILITY

Having clarified that vulnerability is not about (or certainly not only about) showing emotions, let's get clear on what vulnerability is, especially in action. I love this high-level definition from Brene Brown: "I define vulnerability as emotional risk, exposure, uncertainty."[18] That's it, and an even simpler definition of being vulnerable is to be human. We all know that none of us are perfect, yet many of us function with a goal to be perfect, to never make mistakes, to always have the right answers and to always have it together. This awareness opens the door to understanding what vulnerability looks like in action.

Here's a short list of some of the things that represent vulnerability in action:

* Not always having all the answers
* Allowing space for other ideas
* Sharing your uncertainties and humanness
* Asking more questions and making fewer statements
* Being open to feedback
* Being present and listening
* Acknowledging mistakes
* Taking personal responsibility for intended *and unintended* impact
* Holding yourself accountable and telling the truth on yourself
* Asking for help or support
* Demonstrating (not speaking) genuine care for people around you *as people* (not just as assets)

As we'll explore in more detail below, each of these typically represent small steps and moments of vulnerability that are keystones to building connection, relationship and trust in your leadership.

## You Don't Have to Have All the Answers

Walt Rakowich is a friend of mine and he's one of the finest people and leaders I've ever met. In 2020 Walt published his first book, *Transfluence: How to Lead with Transformative Influence in Today's Climates of Change* (Post Hill Press 2020), in which Walt shares his perspectives and philosophies on leadership. The foundation of Walt's message comes from his real-life experience of leading Prologis, the world's largest owner of industrial warehouses, back from the brink of bankruptcy during the Great Recession. As Walt shares in *Transfluence*, one of the keys to his leadership and this momentous turnaround was transparency and vulnerability, as well as a commitment to keeping their people first.

Walt shares the story of being in a late night (actually, early morning) meeting with his finance team and being informed they had just a few weeks before they'd blow $6-7 billion in bond covenants, and they didn't have a solution. He was then informed that if Prologis defaulted on the bond covenants, they'd have to file bankruptcy. When Walt heard this information, he was overwhelmed and felt his face getting white, so he asked everyone to take a short break. When he left the conference room, he realized that he was about to faint and tried to get to a chair to sit down, but he didn't make it.

In other words, Walt was facing a monumental challenge which was so uncomfortable and unsettling that it had a physical impact on him. And this discomfort brought him to a decision point as to whether he would choose to be unsettled, lean into the discomfort and shake up his own leadership by choosing vulnerability in this leadership crisis.

Walt fainted, hit his head on the corner of a desk and literally knocked himself out. When he "came to" minutes later, he was on the floor, his head was cut open and there was blood on the ground around his head. He then realized that the group was waiting for him in the conference room, so he cleaned himself up and went back into the meeting—cut and goose egg visible. After briefly telling his team the story about his fainting, Walt went on to address the fast-approaching financial issue in a company that was already in crisis:

> "And I got to tell you, I was hired to be the CEO of the company and have all the answers, and I got no answer. I said, I had no earthly idea what to do. And you know, what was really interesting, the power of vulnerability is incredible. It's incredibly powerful. I'm not saying leaders should always be vulnerable. You can't, if you are vulnerable all the time, then people begin to question whether or not you should be in the position. You have to make some decisions. But every once in a while, it's actually quite powerful. In that case, it was really interesting. I looked around the room. I had no answers. So I was looking around. I was like, who does have the answer here? Right? All of a sudden, somebody pipes up and said, you know what? 'Walt we're with you, we get it, man. We're in this together. This isn't about, you know,

you having all the answers. We, we got all the answers. We just have to work together to do it.' And I […] realized I'm like, yeah, as a CEO, your job is to empower and lift up and encourage, right? And motivate. But your job isn't always to have all the answers."[19]

Walt saw this as a moment of truth—does he pretend to have all the answers even when he doesn't, or does he model vulnerability by telling the truth? In doing so, Walt created a "we" environment where the collective leadership works together to find the solutions.

Leaders must exercise discernment (not discretion) about when it's the right or best time to be vulnerable, remembering that there will likely be resistance to vulnerability (especially in the beginning). Thus, the resistance can feel like a voice that's saying, "This is the wrong time for vulnerability," when vulnerability is precisely what's needed and what's most uncomfortable or even scary in that moment. This is why self-awareness is such an important part of your leadership growth and edge, especially since self-awareness is a key to enhancing your authentic leadership discernment.

## Make Room for Feedback

It's also important to add one more layer of the Walt Rakowich story. Walt shared with me that shortly after returning to Prologis as the CEO, he initiated a 360-feedback process for his senior leadership team. One key piece of feedback was that Walt's team scored him low on empathy, which is shocking because Walt is one of the most empathetic people and leaders I have ever met. Walt was surprised too, but he was open to the feedback and discovered that because he was going so fast in his efforts to rescue the business, he wasn't taking time for people. Critically, Walt was open to the feedback and took steps to adjust his time and attention to his people. This is another clear example of vulnerability—the request for feedback, the openness to hear difficult feedback and the willingness to take action and make changes in response to the feedback despite being in troubled waters with the business.

One key point is to recognize that Walt's vulnerability had nothing to do with emotions other than his willingness to move through his fears (e.g. the fear of what people will think if he didn't have all the answers). Yes, there were risks in everything that Walt did and said, and vulnerability is the willingness to do and say what he felt was right and true *despite the risks*. This is vulnerability in action, and borrowing Walt's words, "the power of vulnerability is incredible."

## ALLOW SPACE FOR OTHER IDEAS

One vulnerability opportunity for leaders is the openness and encouragement of the ideas of others. Let's face it—in many situations, the top leader's ideas may be better than other ideas because they've likely had more experience with the challenges and solutions. However, that doesn't mean that their "best" ideas are needed for every situation. One thing I tell leaders is that often the "best" solution is your team member's idea even if you believe that it's not actually the best idea. If your people's ideas are not allowed to be implemented, they'll cease offering ideas. After all, who wants to keep offering solutions if the regular message is that their idea isn't good enough. I'm not suggesting that you ignore the best solutions, but I am suggesting that the "best" solutions are often unknown and that there are many opportunities to allow your team members' ideas to be pursued with minimal risks. And remember, taking risks is the essence of vulnerability.

## ASK MORE QUESTIONS

Let's explore a few more tangible ways that leaders can model vulnerability. Most of us are more comfortable making statements, telling people what to do, sharing ideas and directing people and situations. It's ultimately a form of control and the opposite of vulnerability. Asking questions is one of the most powerful leadership and management tools, and it requires vulnerability. Letting go of the need to control the moment, a situation or a conversation is an act of vulnerability. When you choose to ask a well-founded question rather than make a controlling statement, you're letting go of control (a risk) and thus modeling vulnerability.

## BE OPEN TO FEEDBACK

Being open to feedback (asking for it and demonstrating an openness to it) is another vital form of leadership vulnerability. It demands a high level of emotional intelligence and awareness to assure that you don't overreact or appear defensive when you receive negative feedback. This is one of the few areas where a leader must be nearly perfect in receiving feedback, especially in the early part of the leadership relationship. Leaders know that the higher you move up in leadership, the more difficult it is to get feedback from the people that work with you. As challenging as downstream feedback is to give and receive, upstream (or even cross-stream) feedback is uniquely challenging. Thus, if you seek out feedback, it's vital that you hear it well, demonstrate openness to it and be willing to take action to at least understand the feedback and potentially adjust your behavior based upon it. If a team member takes the risk of offering feedback (vulnerability by the team member) and they sense that you're defensive or not open to it, they won't come back with more feedback and you may not get a second chance. Over time, if you've earned enough trust, you may be forgiven for an occasional poor reaction to feedback, but in the beginning, you must make it safe for people to give you rich feedback. We'll talk more about feedback in Chapter 10.

## BEING PRESENT & LISTENING

While it may seem like an unusual version of vulnerability, being present with other people and really listening to them with a genuine interest and curiosity is an important vulnerability practice. Being fully present for another person requires vulnerability, which is why many leaders struggle with being present—the struggle is being both vulnerable and being present. In my prior book, *Just One Step: Walking Backwards to the Present on the Camino Trail*, I highlighted this connection between presence and vulnerability:

> "Now we come to an unexpected and very large obstacle to presence – in order to be present with someone else, you must be willing to be vulnerable. This is a particularly

challenging obstacle to presence because so many of us resist and even reject the idea of being vulnerable with another person. However, if you want to be more present, you must be willing to be more vulnerable." [20]

As Brene Brown has emphasized, vulnerability is the linchpin of connection and a sense of belonging, and the best way to open the door to connection and relationship is to commit to and offer someone the experience of your full presence. In previous books, I've referred to this as the greatest gift we can give another human being—to allow them to experience feeling like the most important person on the planet while you're with them—and this gift creates an environment for mutually vulnerable conversations. This is not about sharing your deepest and darkest secrets, although it could be if enough trust is built. It's simply a conversation where both people are demonstrating their humanness with what they share and the ways they listen to each other.

## Acknowledge Mistakes

Another impactful and trust-building act of vulnerability is acknowledging your mistakes, missteps and errors. We live in a world where such acknowledgements are few and far between, so leaders who are willing to accept responsibility and simply say "I made a mistake" or "I messed up" quickly build trust and influence through these acts of vulnerability. We all make mistakes, but many leaders spend their time and energy ignoring, deflecting or even redirecting responsibility (i.e. blaming others). This breaks down or destroys trust. The opposite behavior is to admit mistakes and take responsibility for the impact of those errors promptly and vulnerably. Leaders who regularly make these admissions build trust because people realize that leaders will make mistakes. What breaks trust is a leader's unwillingness to admit it, or even worse, blaming other people or circumstances for the outcomes.

## TAKE RESPONSIBILITY

We'll talk more about taking personal responsibility for impacts (both intentional and unintentional) in Chapter 11, but for now it's critical to understand that this is one of the most often-missed opportunities for vulnerability. The lack of impact responsibility is also one of the biggest contributors to breaking and diminishing trust. For now, just plant the seed inside your mind that vulnerable and therefore trustworthy leaders are not only willing, but quick to accept personal responsibility for the impacts that their words and actions have on others—*even if, and especially if, that impact was unintended.*

Team members are tired of hearing their leaders say things like, "That's not what I meant" or "That's not what I intended" when they become aware of an unintended impact that has affected their team. It's dismissive of the team member's experience and sends a strong message that the team member should ignore the impact (or get over it) just because it wasn't intended. Essentially, it communicates to a team member that the impact doesn't matter, and therefore, they don't matter. Vulnerability in the form of taking impact responsibility is the cure for this massive trust and influence buster.

## ACCOUNTABILITY

Before we move on in this leadership journey, let's look at the final three key acts of vulnerability. Accountability is one of the biggest challenges for any organization or team for two reasons. First, most people are focused on improving the ways and the degree to which they hold other people accountable, which is the wrong focus and approach. Don't worry, we'll go deep into accountability in Chapters 8 and 9. The second reason is most people think they're more accountable and self-accountable than they actually are.

Like with most things in leadership, we don't decide for ourselves how accountable we are—other people decide. While you do decide if you feel in integrity with yourself, other people decide if you're accountable and can be trusted to consistently deliver on your commitments. Other people also decide if you're being responsible and taking ownership for the impact of your lack of accountability.

Imagine this scenario within a team: the leader makes a commitment to a person, group or the entire team. Instead of pretending it didn't happen, deflecting it or blaming someone or something else, that leader steps up in some public fashion and says something like this:

> I made a commitment to get back to Sarah with some important information by Noon today. I didn't honor that commitment. What I chose to do, instead, was to prioritize my work over the information Sarah needed. The impact on Sarah of me not honoring my commitment is that she wasn't able to finish her report (as she'd committed to John), which impacted the project and potentially her relationship with John. Another impact is that Sarah likely trusts me less to honor my commitments. I feel like I've let Sarah and the team down. This is not the type of leader that I want to be, and I'm committed to doing better! One way I can do better in the future is to have more proactive communication with Sarah and everyone about commitments I've made. I intend to do better in the future and I'm fully open to your feedback going forward when I don't demonstrate these improvements.

What happens to trust when a leader is willing to be this vulnerable with his team and team members? Unless the old behavior continues, trust is catapulted and the team is likely to be more fully committed to the leader and the mission.

## Ask for Support

The next act of vulnerability is often the most difficult to exercise, and therefore one of the most important. The simple act of asking for help or support. When I ask audiences how many people feel like they do well in helping others or *giving* help, nearly every hand quickly goes up. However, when I then follow up by asking who's great at *asking* for help, it's rare that even five percent of the hands go up and they go up slowly. Why are we better at giving help than asking for help? Simple—because we have a false narrative that asking for help is a sign of weakness, much like what we typically believe about vulnerability. To be clear, this belief is false but that doesn't mean that some people still think that asking for help is a sign of weakness (for themselves or from others). Thus, this is the risk involved in asking for help which makes it an act of vulnerability.

Walt Rakowich modeled this form of vulnerability in the preceding story when he admitted that he didn't have all the answers. I am often reminded of a scene in the movie *Remember the Titans* (2000). Will Patton's character, Coach Yoast, always insisted that he didn't need help. In one scene he turns to Denzel Washington's character, Coach Boone, and says, "Herman, I sure could use your help." This tiny moment and statement are giant acts of vulnerability between the two coaches, and it opened the door to levels of trust, connection and relationship with immense positive impact.

## CARING & EMPATHY

Finally, the demonstration (not just words) of genuine care, concern and empathy (not sympathy, which is different) for your team members as people (not just assets of the organization) is an impactful form of vulnerability. While it may not seem like a risk like many of the other vulnerability acts discussed earlier in this chapter, the risk is in bringing down the walls of "let's keep this strictly business" and baring our mutual humanness with each other. Lowering your guard also means letting other people "in." There's a false belief that leaders can't let anyone get close to them nor should they become close to anyone else. This, however, leads to team members feeling disconnected from leaders and judging that the leader is cold, unempathetic and uncaring.

While we'll talk more about empathy throughout this book, remember that empathy is not the same as a lack of boundaries. I've often and even recently heard leaders say that you have to "be careful not to be too empathetic," but this is simply wrong. While we can be too *sympathetic*, we can't ever be too *empathetic*—they're very different. As Walt Rakowich shares:

"And you realize, man, these people are living with their personal lives, as well as their business lives. […] So, when you think about being a leader, if you weren't empathetic during that time, something's wrong. And part of empathy is not having answers and you know, not like 'let me tell you where we're going to go.' It's listening. And listening and processing take some form of vulnerability. I think, you know, that perhaps they have something more to say than you. And I think that in many respects, leaders should not expect their flock to come to them and tell them all of their difficulties right now. I don't think that's happening. I think they need to be the people that are processing or that are opening up other people to talk about the things that they're, you know, concerned about. So, you know, in this environment, empathy and flexibility matter. Not necessarily carrying the flag over the goal line and saying, 'follow me.' I don't think that that's what we need today now. … I'm not saying that leaders shouldn't lead. I am saying that leaders should lead with more empathy today. Leaders should listen more before they react and carry that flag."[21]

What a powerful and team empowering statement about the importance of vulnerability and empathy in leadership, especially today.

## Opening the Kimono

We started off this chapter referencing the need to get naked in your leadership by exposing yourself to the risks of being human, and hopefully, you're leaving this chapter with a clearer sense of two things:

1.  What vulnerability is and is not
2.  How vital vulnerability is in leadership

Make no mistake about it—vulnerability is a risk, and as highlighted earlier, external and modeled vulnerability requires internal vulnerability (the willingness to take the risks). This is what Brene Brown defines as courage, and we all know that leadership requires courage.

Talk about shaking things up and internal disruption. We live in a world today where vulnerability is often the most likely leadership trait to be avoided or ignored. Choosing to model vulnerability as a leader is "crazy" in the current state of business and leadership, yet that craziness is precisely the disruption that's needed to close the ever-widening leadership gap. Your people—the people you are tasked and empowered to lead—are looking to experience your humanness so that they can trust you and choose to follow you based upon that trust. The question today is not whether we need to shake up leadership with more vulnerability; the truer question is whether you'll choose to take the risks of shaking up your own snow globe by embracing vulnerability as a core ingredient in your disruptive and essential leadership.

If you're still not convinced of the essential role of vulnerability in leadership, consider this metaphor. Imagine building a brick wall around yourself which only has an opening for people to hear your words. This brick wall will likely keep you safe from the risk of being physically wounded, but it won't protect you from the possibility of being emotionally wounded. At the same time, the brick wall will keep you separated and disconnected from people. They won't really see you or know you other than for your words, and you'll have successfully kept yourself physically safe while still being subject to potential emotional injury (often self-inflicted). In other words, you don't really get the protection you want, and you'll certainly pay the price of disconnection, lack of relationship and an absence of trust. Yes, the brick wall (lack of vulnerability) will lower but not eliminate the risks of vulnerability, but it's at a very high cost to you, your leadership, your relationships, your influence and your impact.

We know that leadership is all about the risks. If there aren't any risks, then leadership isn't required. If there's no uncertainty, then leadership isn't required. If anyone and everyone can do it, leadership isn't required. I'm often reminded of a profound exchange in the movie *A League of their Own* (1992), when Tom Hanks' character, Jimmy Dugan, and Gina Davis' character, Dottie Hinson, are discussing her reason for leaving the team. Dottie tells Jimmy that "It just got too hard." To which Jimmy replies, "It's supposed to be hard. If it was easy, everyone would do it. The hard is what makes it great." I often think of leadership the same way … it's the hard, the risky, the uncertain that makes it great. In this case, it's the vulnerability that's required in leadership that's challenging, risky and hard—that's why leadership is a choice, but vulnerability is NOT a choice if you want to be a trustworthy, impactful and influential leader.

# Chapter 5

# We've Got You

Do YOU REMEMBER learning how to ride a bike? If you're close to my age, your memory may be a little fuzzy, but you'll likely remember teaching your own children how to ride a bike. Whether you remember your own experience, your experience with your children or are just using simple logic, you know well that the best way to teach someone to ride a bike involves five fundamental elements:

1. Patience
2. Guidance / Instruction
3. Support and Encouragement
4. Failure Management
5. Safety

While learning to ride a bike usually doesn't take a long time, it certainly requires patience because you (the teacher) know how to ride the bike and your student doesn't. Guidance and instruction are critical because it's more than just saying, "All you have to do is pedal and balance."

The support comes in two forms—verbal and physical. The physical support is when the teacher typically runs alongside the student and holds the back of the seat. In other words, the teacher is WITH the student on the journey, physically and verbally. The verbal support nearly always comes down to communicating these three things:

1. "You can do it."
2. "I've got you."
3. "You'll be okay."

The failure management element is obvious since you can't keep running alongside and holding your child or team forever. Eventually you have to let go (gradually) and let them fall, because falling (failing) is what allows them to learn about balance and to learn the edges of their balance.

The final foundation (safety) is obvious and includes running alongside and holding the seat. The key is to set them up to fail safely in order to learn without extreme outcomes. Certainly, most of you would never teach someone to ride a bike by giving them the basic instructions, putting them at the top of a hill with a busy highway at the bottom, and telling them to make sure they don't fall or ride into the traffic. No, you typically let them ride alone on the grass or another soft spot so they can "fail" safely. Then you allow them to fall on the sidewalk—rougher but still safe learning. Eventually you let them ride in the street, and they'll again fall in a relatively controlled environment. In other words, you allow them to fail so that they can learn and grow, while staying relatively safe.

If you haven't yet figured it out, teaching someone to ride a bike is both literal and metaphorical. Yes, it's the literal way to teach someone to ride a bike. It's also a metaphor for the most effective way to grow and develop your people. Most important for this chapter, it's a metaphor for perhaps the most critical objective for leaders in any organization—creating a culture of safety (physical, mental, emotional and psychological). Thus, the chapter title of "We've Got You."

## WHAT IS SAFETY?

For decades, safety in the workplace has been limited to providing for the physical safety of your team members. In the United States for example, the Occupational Safety and Health Administration ("OSHA") and the related Occupational Safety and Health Act came into existence in 1970 (just over fifty years ago) to "assure safe and healthy working conditions for working men and women by setting and enforcing standards and by providing training, outreach, education and assistance."[22] Certainly there was, and remains, a critical need to provide for the physical safety of your team and in the workplace, and this need was highlighted during the COVID pandemic.

Virtually overnight, organizations and leaders were faced with making potentially life and death decisions regarding their team members. Rather than focusing on team questions like engagement and performance, the fundamental question was "In what ways can we keep our people safe while continuing to do business?" Notably, many of you as leaders were, for the first time, making physical safety decisions regarding your team members. In addition to assuring business survival, the two fundamental questions were "In what ways can we keep our people safe while continuing to operate business as almost usual?" (essential businesses) or "In what ways can we keep our people safe while working remotely?" And yet, with all this focus on safety, the issues of physical safety took priority over emotional, psychological and mental health.

While some organizations and leaders have given thought and attention to team mental health during the COVID pandemic—perhaps due to the extreme nature of the pandemic's psychological impact[23]— the concept of creating a culture of safety within an organization often remains largely overlooked or minimized. In fact, the concept is relatively new and has been amplified by thought leader and motivational speaker Simon Sinek, who has this to say:

> "By creating a Circle of Safety around the people in the organization, leadership reduces the threats people feel inside the group, which frees them up to focus more time and energy to protect the organization from the constant

dangers outside and seize the big opportunities. Without a Circle of Safety, people are forced to spend too much time and energy protecting themselves from each other."[24]

"Protecting themselves from each other"? At first glance, that concept feels absurd, but we all know what this means and it's certain that you've either experienced this lack of security yourself or witnessed team members who needed this protection.

As noted above, physical safety is, and will always be, a priority in the workplace. However, it's time to embrace a wider and more holistic model of workplace safety which includes emotional, psychological, mental AND physical work-wellbeing. There are many facets that foster a culture of security in an organization.

Here's a starting list of examples that can broaden our perspectives of safety at work:

- Safety from verbal abuse
- Safety from shaming
- Safety from backstabbing
- Safety from harassment of any kind
- Safety from biased / different treatment (or mistreatment)
- Safety from inequity
- Safety from being thrown under the bus
- Safety from being overworked and burned out
- Safety from bullying, including emotional intimidation
- Safety from being ignored
- Safety from manipulation
- Safety from exploitation
- Safety from politics
- Safety from isolation
- Safety from discrimination
- Safety from silent judgment

* Safety from dehumanization
* Safety from microaggressions

And that list may be just a beginning.

It's likely that you have one of two reactions to this expansive list. If you're a team member, your reaction is likely, "A work environment like that would be amazing." If you're a leader in the organization, your reaction is likely, "That's overwhelming. How are we supposed to accomplish that?" Or "Why is this my / our job?" We'll shortly address these questions, but for the moment, I want you to imagine the many ways that your workplace, team, engagement levels, performance and outcomes would benefit with this level of safety.

Safety is where our most important measure of success comes into play. For decades, we've focused our energies and efforts on assessing and increasing the return on investment. Even when it comes to investing in our people, we tend to evaluate and ponder our potential return on that investment. If you haven't clearly realized the importance of a culture of safety during the pandemic, then you haven't been paying attention. Understanding the essential nature found in a culture of safety is not limited to the pandemic or other crisis—there's an incomprehensible return when you shift your focus to assessing, obsessing and investing in your *Return on Safety*.

Just imagine how different your workplace and organization would be with a clear and actionized commitment to enhancing your return on safety (ROS). How much would your team and employee engagement grow? What would be the positive impact on communication, teamwork and accountability? Consider the acceleration in performance, execution and achieving your goals and objectives? Here's the deepest truth: as you increase your ROS, you'll simultaneously and exponentially increase your profitability, consistency and impact.

Simon Sinek offers this on the impact of building a culture of safety:

> "When a leader makes the choice to put the safety and lives of the people inside the organization first, to sacrifice their comforts and sacrifice the tangible results, so that the people remain and feel safe and feel like they belong, remarkable things happen."[25]

Sinek continues that "When we feel safe inside the organization, we will naturally combine our talents and our strengths and work tirelessly to face the dangers outside and seize the opportunities."[26] How's that for a return on safety?

Hopefully, you've heard enough to: a.) believe in the power, value and impact of creating a culture of safety, and to b.) relentlessly pursue and continue improving your return on safety. We'll be exploring this culture of safety topic below and in the coming chapters, and Chapters 3 (trust) and 4 (vulnerability) are key foundations to creating and nurturing a culture of safety. For now, just hold close the notion that safety at work means so much more than physical safety and that this expanded version of safety (when achieved) will transform organizations, families and lives.

*Safety at work means so much more than physical safety.*

## OBJECTIONS TO SAFETY

Not surprisingly, there are, and will be, oppositions to creating cultures of safety and focusing on the return on safety. This is why we opened by referencing the need to assure that your people experience the message "we've got you." These people typically communicate with three types of attitudes:

1. Stuck in the Past: "Holistic safety was not a topic or issue when I was getting into the workplace."

2. Abdication: "Why is it my / our job to provide this broader safety to our team?"

3. Doubt: "How am I / are we supposed to achieve this expanded vision of safety?"

All good questions, but they can be dealt with rather simply.

## Looking Ahead:

First, yes, it's true—emotional and other safety weren't part of the business and workplace conversation until the past ten or fifteen years. All the focus has been on the obvious topic of physical safety because it's crystal clear why physical safety is important. However, we know that for decades, physical safety was not a priority in the workplace and tens of thousands of people in the United States alone were injured or died in workplace accidents. Why? Because *at that time,* the accepted mindset was largely profits over people and employees were viewed as expendable. But times, priorities, employee expectations and markets changed and *then* physical safety became a priority.

Over the past decade or so, a similar shift has occurred, where the focus beyond physical safety is gaining visibility, acceptance and expectancy. Today's teams and team members, especially millennials, the largest generation in the workplace today at 35%,[27] are speaking with their engagement, or lack thereof, and are demanding a culture of holistic safety from their organizations.[28] Thus, while building cultures of safety is a relatively new concept, the company's well-being is essential in moving forward in order to achieve all of your organizational and team goals … especially if and when you commit to putting your people first.

## Ownership of the Team:

Secondly, it comes down to three truths in terms of why it's the organization's "job" to provide a broader sense of security to and for our team members:

1. As noted above, teams and team members are demanding it and they're speaking with either their engagement, performance or their feet.

2. Failure to provide a culture of safety sends a clear message that you don't care about or value your people (again impacting engagement, performance and retention).

3. Work is the place where people spend the largest percentage of their time in their lives, especially once you factor out sleep.

I could go on explaining these three truths, but it's not really necessary. As I learned in my lawyering days, *res ipsa loquitor*, Latin for "the thing speaks for itself", and in this context the points listed above speak for themselves.

If you have any doubts about the foregoing and the fact that people are rethinking work and life, then witness what's being called the Great Resignation (or perhaps the great reassessment). From April through June of 2021, 11.5 million workers in the United States voluntarily quit. While many business owners are quick to suggest that the reason is laziness and unemployment benefits, the research suggests otherwise. Here's what one writer offered regarding the Great Resignation and a LinkedIn survey:

> "There are numerous reasons, most originating from the pandemic that started in early '20. According to a LinkedIn survey, 74% of respondents said the time spent at home had caused them to rethink their current work situation. More than 50% cited stress and burnout in their job as a reason for looking elsewhere. Others did not like how their employer treated them over the last eighteen months, from a lack of genuine concern to employees being forced to take concessions, while senior executives didn't. The Work from Home (WFH) dilemma opened a pandora's box for many employees and has become a contentious issue for many organizations. And finally, yes, the increase in unemployment benefits has caused a lack of urgency for many to return to the workforce."[29]

These are the realities of these times and the future, and the only question is whether leaders and organizations are rethinking work to the same degree that the workforce is rethinking work.

## BELIEF:

Now we come to the *how*—how we can achieve this expanded vision and concept of safety. We'll be covering this throughout the book since every topic discussed, previously and going forward, supports a people-first culture and culture of safety. Making a commitment matters more in this moment than figuring out each of the components needed to create a safe workplace. Ideally, it's important to make a public commitment and proclamation to your team and team members that you, as a leader, believe in a culture of safety and will be accountable in taking actions and making decisions to create, nurture and sustain such a culture. If that feels scary, then good—you've found a key leadership edge and its decision time. This is precisely the type of vulnerability that's needed in leadership—the willingness to get beyond the ways you've always thought and led, as well as committing to your team's well-being more fully and deeply than ever before. That's what happens when you choose to shake things up and disrupt your own leadership.

Will you make and deliver on a promise of a culture of safety and make the return on safety as high a priority (or even higher) than all others in your organization? Or will you continue to lead and do business as you have in the past? Do you want to continue to settle with the engagement, results and performance that you've achieved in the past, all the while leaving your people to suffer through their emotional, psychological and mental challenges on their own?

Which leader will you choose to be?

## Achieving Safety

Make no mistake … the idea of creating a culture of safety can feel complicated and overwhelming, but there's a simplicity that we can grab onto, founded upon the simple idea of treating people as people, not assets. The unspoken philosophy in this concept is that you're consciously committing to putting your people first and you're consistently putting that commitment into action. What if that's all a culture of safety is really all about?

Simon Sinek has said that "Leadership is about making people feel safe. When someone feels heard, they feel safe." Could it be that simple—assuring that people feel heard? Let's try this theory out in terms of investing time in our people. When we make time for our people, people feel seen, heard, valued and that they matter. When we fail to make time for our people, people feel unseen, unheard, unvalued and as if they don't matter. Is there really any argument to these truths?

Similarly, if we're committed to putting our people first and understand that leadership is all about our people, wouldn't we naturally, albeit sometimes imperfectly, provide a culture that offers all the elements of safety listed above? If we authentically put our people first because we care about our team members, then we'd establish and hold boundaries around all the safety desires listed above. We would declare and hold zero tolerance boundaries in all of the areas where people might feel unsafe.

We would never say things like "That's just how [insert name] is" if that person's behavior diminishes safety. Rather than saying things like "That's not what I meant," we would take full responsibility for the impact we have and commit with action to diminishing and then eliminating the behavior and the impact in the future. We would model a culture of safety with our own behavior and actions while also holding high standards for the entire team to align with those behaviors and actions. We would make it clear that maintaining a culture of safety is an expectation for the organization, the leaders and every team member and we would communicate, act, decide and lead in alignment with that expectation and commitment. In short, we would humanize our leadership and our organization, all the while leading with an assurance that relationships, trust and safety are the non-negotiable foundations.

We'll talk more about the role and impact of tolerance in Chapter 12, but for now just note that your tolerance factor is the primary driver and measure of our organization's culture, especially when it comes to building a culture of safety. While we're often well intentioned about how we take care of our team, we fail to align our decisions and actions with those intentions, thus creating massive cracks in whatever people-focused culture we say we desire. When it comes to physical activities, we often say that we need to put our backs into it, but when it comes to building and nurturing a culture of safety, the more appropriate expectation is that we need to put our hearts into it. This is why a culture of safety is more an outcome of our authentic, heartful and accountable commitments to our people, so long as we're willing to vulnerably risk trying out the people-first wisdom. Talk about an essential leadership disruption.

# MENTAL HEALTH AT WORK

Before we move on from the culture of safety and return on safety, it's important that we spend a few moments addressing one of the biggest objections and elephants in the room. Too often, leaders and organizations take the position that their peoples' mental health is not their responsibility. Instead, they argue that people need to be responsible for their own mental health. Certainly, each person must take personal responsibility for whatever mental health challenges and opportunities they have in their lives. However, the reality is that people today spend more time working (whether at the office or at home) than they do anything else. Given this reality, organizations and the workplace are uniquely positioned to not only avoid increasing people's stress and anxiety, but to also be part of the solution.

We have a mental health crisis in the United States and the COVID pandemic amplified this crisis because of the wide range of chaos and uncertainty that it created for people, professionally and personally. As an organization and leader in that organization, you have three (3) basic mindset choices to make when it comes to your people:

1. Our people's mental health is neither our problem nor our responsibility.

2. Our responsibility to our people is to minimize or eliminate any *additional* mental health impact.

3. Our responsibility and opportunity is to provide a culture and workplace experience that *increases and improves* our people's mental health.

What's your reaction to each of these options? Which option feels like leadership? Which option feels like servant leadership? Which option will best impact what you claim to stand for as an organization and leader? You may not yet have a clear path on how to specifically achieve a culture of safety, but the path follows the commitment and it's not necessary to know the path in order to make the commitment.

If this all feels overwhelming and perhaps crazy, remember these inspirational words from Apple's "here's to the crazy ones" marketing campaign in 1997:

> "Here's to the crazy ones. The misfits. The rebels. The troublemakers. The round pegs in the square holes. The ones who see things differently.
>
> They're not fond of rules.
>
> And they have no respect for the status quo.
>
> You can quote them, disagree with them, glorify or vilify them. About the only thing you can't do is ignore them. Because they change things. They push the human race forward.
>
> While some may see them as the crazy ones, we see genius. Because the people who are crazy enough to think they can change the world, are the ones who do."

What a beautiful example of the concepts we've already discussed—being willing to disrupt, getting naked (vulnerability), taking risks and refusing to settle—living out a leader's commitment to shaking things up and creating impacts and outcomes beyond what you've previously experienced.

As we've learned throughout history, the right thing often feels crazy and uncertain. The same is true when it comes to putting your team and colleagues first, and more specifically, building and nurturing a culture of safety. Just imagine the ways your teams would collaborate, communicate and execute in a safe environment. Imagine the ways your team members would grow and develop within such a culture. Imagine the positive impact your organization, team, clients and customers, innovation, revenues and profitability would experience in a culture of safety.

If you're feeling like this mindset is above and beyond the ways you've envisioned leadership in the past, you're right and that's the nature of snow globe shaking leadership. It IS about creating, innovating, engaging and supporting beyond what you've likely previously imagined. It IS about shifting from offering well-being programs to making a commitment to a well-being culture. It IS about breathing life into your people and culture. It IS about leaping in your leadership. It IS about bringing more humanity to your leadership, culture and organization. As one leadership thought leader recently suggested, "the great resignation continues to elevate our need for humanity at work."[30]

## THE SAFETY CHOICE

Achieving a culture of safety begins with a commitment and while the tactics may get complicated, there's a simplicity to the path—put your people first and treat them accordingly. All of this comes down to a choice, even if you don't know where to start. Simon Sinek famously offered the following:

> "*Leadership is a choice.* It is not a rank. I know many people at the senior most levels of organizations who are absolutely not leaders. They are authorities, and we do what they say because they have authority over us, but we would not follow them. And I know many people who are at the bottoms of organizations who have no authority and they are absolutely leaders, and this is because they have chosen to look after the person to the left of them, and they have chosen to look after the person to the right of them. This is what a leader is."[31]

A culture of safety is much the same—it begins with a choice, followed by a commitment, and reinforced and sculpted with decisions, boundaries and actions in alignment with the choice and commitment. As you continue your journey through this book, focus more on the commitment and know that YOUR choice as a leader matters and trust that sustaining a culture of safety for your people will always pay off in impact and outcomes beyond your imagination.

# Chapter 6

# Mind Your Gaps

IF YOU'VE EVER traveled to London, you'll be familiar with these signs you see everywhere on The Tube (London's underground railway system):

> **Mind the Gap**
>
> Please, mind the gap between the train and the platform

The first time I saw these signs, there was something familiar about them, and then it hit me—the signs remind me of the leadership gaps (aka blind spots) that we have. One of the most fundamental blind spots or gaps is our overestimation of how well we're doing, whether in leadership, communication, engagement, customer experience, etc. No matter the topic, we invariably overestimate our abilities or performance, which creates leadership gaps in turn.

To match our leadership realities, a great way to reframe the signs in London is as follows:

## Mind the Gap

Please, mind the gap between *self-perception and reality*

The foundational truth is that perception is reality when it comes to people (yes, we're all humans). We often come to believe our own perceptions to be true, especially when we're not open and rarely listen to the perspectives and perceptions of others.

## CRITICAL GAPS AND BLIND SPOTS

Some years ago, while working with a construction business, I came across one giant blind spot or gap. As you might know, one top priority in all construction businesses is safety and this was a regular topic of conversation for this client. More specifically, the business appeared to be excelling with safety, yet I often heard stories that made me question whether I misunderstood safety or there was a safety gap.

During a meeting involving key leaders, I asked them to list all the areas in the business that needed attention (e.g., areas of the business that were not functioning well). Notably, safety wasn't mentioned, but I took the risk and asked two questions on safety:

1.  Based on how you promote and talk about safety, what's your safety performance assessment? *The answer was 95%, meaning that they needed to work on improving this 5% gap.*

2.  What's the honest assessment of your safety performance? *Everyone kept quiet for several minutes, and then one senior*

*leader spoke up and expressed his concerns about safety. He addressed the issue of talking a better game than delivering. The group then agreed that their safety performance was more like 80%, and they still needed to work on the additional 20% gap.*

This is when it hit me—how overestimating our performance (e.g., lack of self-awareness, lack of self-honesty, ego) sets us up to fail at achieving our objectives.

The simple leadership and business truth I learned from this conversation is:

A five percent (5%) solution won't solve a twenty percent (20%) gap, *but a twenty percent (20%) solution WILL solve a five percent (5%) gap.*

In other words, if the assessment of our gaps, challenges and opportunities is underestimated, it's highly unlikely we'll achieve our objectives using our ideas and solutions. However, if we overestimate our gaps, innovate and solve for a larger gap, it's highly LIKELY we'll achieve our objectives using our ideas and solutions.

Here are the takeaways from this conversation about minding our gaps:

- You and your team are never as good as you think
- Overestimate your gaps so that your solutions will solve your actual gaps
- A 10% solution won't solve a 20% problem
- A 20% solution will solve a 10% problem

As we discussed in Chapter 2, we noticed this same gap in other areas, including assessing our own leadership. As Tommy Spaulding shared in a Leadership Junkies podcast episode, "In twenty years of this business, I've never had anybody ever say to me, you know Tommy, 'I'm a self-serving leader,' so basically 90% of people call themselves servant leaders yet only 10% really are."[32] Think about it – how many times have you heard a positional leader say something like, "I know I'm a terrible leader, but I don't care."

The more I've explored the foundations of leadership, I've concluded that one of the biggest gaps and blind spots is not that we don't believe in what it takes to be an influential, trustworthy and impactful leader, but we think we're already leading in these ways. If you think you've largely already arrived as a leader or that you just need some tweaks in your leadership, you're not likely to be open to feedback. You're also unlikely to invest much time, energy or focus on improving what you believe you're already excelling at.

## A Gaping Gap

One of the biggest gaps I've experienced in leadership relates to personal ownership and responsibility—specifically the concept of extreme ownership, which permeates team conversations today. The spark that lit this flame was the book *Extreme Ownership: How U.S. Navy SEALs Lead and Win* (St. Martin's Press 2015) by Jocko Willink and Leif Babin. The foundation of extreme ownership is the idea that leadership at all levels is vital, and part of that leadership requires each person to take 100% responsibility for every outcome. Thus, if each person takes full responsibility, then each person is asking the question, "In what ways can I do something different in the future to impact the outcome positively?" Rather than work to allocate responsibility, the extreme ownership mindset invites each person to take 100% responsibility for the outcome, not just their own decisions and actions.

As simple as this concept appears, it's fertile ground for a massive leadership gap.

A few years ago, I met with the CEO of a large insurance business— he had recently read the book *Extreme Ownership*. He was excited about bringing its principles into his organization. A few minutes later, he mentioned an issue he was having with one of his senior leaders and the CEO said, "I've owned my part of the issue and he needs to own his part." In response, I asked him if he'd actually read *Extreme Ownership* since there's no such concept as parts of ownership. Even though he had read about extreme ownership—owning all of it and always examining what you could have done differently to impact the outcome—he'd interpreted extreme ownership as taking full ownership of his *half of the issue.* This CEO is not the only one who has a blind spot when it comes to ownership and responsibility.

For years now, I've been using this visual in presentations to highlight this blind spot.

When it comes to taking full ownership of issues and outcomes, we typically think of allocating 100% of responsibility relative to each issue or outcome. Think about the times when you've argued with someone and you say something like, "I've owned my part. You need to own your part."

The miss or blind spot is the reality that whenever an issue or an outcome fails to meet expectations, the number of responsibility circles is equal to the number of people involved in the situation. For example, if five (5) people are involved in a miscommunication or misunderstanding, then the circles of responsibility will look like this:

*Each person* has one circle of full ownership. Embracing this level of full personal ownership and responsibility will profoundly improve your levels of communication, understanding, accountability, commitment, execution and impact. It also requires a fundamental shift past a likely prior blind spot so each person is empowered and expected to always look for ways to impact the outcomes in the future differently. While seemingly simple, this is a disruptive shift since it's contrary to the ways many of us have been looking at ownership for years.

Your ego is often the driver of your blind spots since it's the voice that tells you everything you think is true. Blind spots exist because of the reality that *none of us knows what we don't know.* The gap between what we consciously know and all the things that we miss is the land of blind spots.

My father's stroke from many years ago and his accompanying loss of peripheral vision is a wonderful metaphor for blind spots. As a result of his stroke, he has limited peripheral vision, resulting in huge blind spots compared to someone with normal peripheral vision. The challenging part is that these literal blind spots for him are not black spots—rather, his brain tells him that he sees the full width of vision that he's used to, but he's actually only seeing a small part of what's actually there. Talk about a blind spot!

The same is true for our own blind spots. We see a situation, issue, problem, event or opportunity as whole and complete, but our humanness has missing elements. These missing elements are our blind spots. For example, I often hear this phrase from leaders: "I'm very aware of my blind spots." Hello … blind spot warning! We can only become aware of what used to be blind spots (albeit unresolved blind spots), but we can't be aware of current blind spots because they are, after all, blind spots.

> *Your ego is often the driver of your blind spots.*

The context where I'm most familiar with blind spots is in driving since I had early knowledge of how dangerous blind spots can be. As a result, I don't like driving with people in my blind spots and I don't want to be in other people's blind spots. As a result, I avoid blind spots, which means that I typically accelerate my car so that I'm no longer in someone else's blind spot and they're no longer in mine. However, here's the critical part, what happens when I accelerate out of a blind spot? *I automatically create a new blind spot.*

There might not be another car in that blind spot right now and I may not be in the blind spot of another driver, but there are always blind spots, and this is a fundamental mindset shake-up and shift for your leadership. Know that there will always be blind spots in your awareness, perspectives and assessments. These blind spots are likely to be your biggest stumbling blocks in every element of your leadership, including communication, relationships, decision making, discernment, innovation, problem-solving and pursuing opportunities. Given the nature of blind spots, we must now address a few strategies to lead through these realities of blind spots.

## FILLING THE GAPS

There are four key strategies for navigating blind spots.

1. Acknowledge the reality of blind spots
2. Follow your misses, surprises and confusion
3. Exaggerate your gaps
4. Bless challengers

The first strategy is simple and obvious—acknowledge that you have and will always have blind spots. While this may seem overly simplistic, it's essential as a starting point because your blind spots will be bigger and more invisible as long as you pretend they don't exist. Think of it like you're running a 100-yard hurdle in the dark without knowing there are hurdles. Talk about getting tripped up. However, if you acknowledge the truth of blind spots even if you don't know them, you can run the race differently and with at least some ambient light to limit your number and degree of stumbles.

The second blind spot strategy involves a high degree of self-awareness and self-reflection by following the clues that come when you miss something, are surprised by a situation or outcome, or are confused by a situation or outcome. Think of a scenario where your reaction is some version of "I didn't see that coming." If so, then it's likely there's a blind spot at work. Similarly, when you cause an impact you didn't anticipate (more on impacts in Chapter 11), you likely have a blind spot related to either the cause or effect of that impact. Our unconscious biases are often a

*Unconscious biases are often a source of blind spots.*

source of blind spots in terms of unintended impact. Whenever you find yourself surprised at an outcome or situation, assume that there's a blind spot in play and explore what blind spots may be impacting your experience and leadership.

One very practical and prevailing blind spot everyone has is the often arrogant belief that everyone else thinks, reacts and feels the same way. In other words, if something doesn't bother me, it won't bother you—if I like receiving feedback in a certain way, you must like receiving feedback the same way—if I prioritize my time a certain way, you must prioritize the same way. Get the point—the often unconscious belief that everyone else is just like you is a blind spot. The good news is that this blind spot is relatively easy to adjust since hopefully, you all know that the belief that everyone is like you is simply not true. Thus, the strategy for this blind spot is nothing more than acknowledging and being open to the fact that not everyone is like you, and thus seeking to listen, learn and understand how others communicate, make decisions, innovate, etc.

The third blind spot strategy is highly effective and is largely based on the belief that we typically think we're better than we are. In the example above regarding safety, if you know that we typically underestimate our gap, then the solution is to exaggerate our gaps and thereby amplify our solutions. As in the example above, a ten percent (10%) solution won't solve a twenty percent (20%) problem, so you must assume that any existing gaps are larger than what you believe they are. The only challenge here is that you may naturally seek to minimize your gaps knowing that you're then going to exaggerate them, but this is simply solved with a little self-awareness and inviting open conversations with and questions from your team members to best assure that you are exaggerating your gaps.

The fourth and final blind spot strategy is perhaps the most frightening and it certainly requires the most amount of vulnerability. I call it blessing challengers in every part of your life. Yes, we certainly need to encourage and be open to honest feedback, but blessing challengers take people's perspectives to a whole new level. It not only raises the bar on the quality and quantity of the feedback, but it clearly and specifically empowers people around you to tell you the truth in statements and invite you to explore the truth using questions.

Make no mistake that this is much more than just asking people to give you feedback. Depending on your existing trust levels, it may require you to first focus on building the relational trust levels to get the honest, rich and robust feedback you need.

Before we get into the blessing mindset and approach, know that there are many types of challengers that you can bless depending on where they fit in the context of your leadership and life. Certainly, you want to include key family members and friends—people who see the deeper truths of you up close and personal. Their perspectives are vital to help you better understand yourself, your triggers and your defaults. You also need to bless challengers at work in the form of team members, colleagues and especially people that report to you. This is the most difficult source from which to get honest feedback, but without it, you'll be leading without even having any "mirrors" to help you with your blind spots.

To really enhance the scope and depth of your feedback and blind spot spotting, you must consider leaning into a mentor or coach who has the benefit of insider knowledge with external experiences and perspectives. It's easier for these people not to be caught up in the dynamics of the existing personal or professional relationships so you can get keen insights into the blind spots that are holding back your leadership.

Now, the final three elements of blessings challengers are blessing, clarity / commitment and perfection. The blessing part is about intentionality and communication. Think about the uniqueness of the concept of blessing as compared to simply asking for feedback. To bless means to fully and vulnerably invite another person to help you see the things you likely can't see on your own. You don't need to use the word "blessing" with someone, but it's important that the nature of your task is empowering and your communication demonstrates your clear commitment to growth (part two).

While a script is not necessary, the following is a good guide for the intention, commitment and vulnerability of your blessing to share with someone:

I've realized that I have blind spots and often think I'm doing better than I actually am when it comes to my leadership. I've also realized that I can't uncover all of my blind spots. I'm committed to become not only more self-aware but more effective as a leader and I can't do this alone. I need two things from you. 1. Your honest and ongoing feedback and input on the ways I show up as a leader, even when I don't ask for it at the moment. 2. Your willingness to remind me when I don't show up the ways I say I want to once I uncover a new blind spot or behavior change. I know this is risky for you, and I hope that you'll take the risk of helping me to continue to learn and grow.

I didn't use the word "blessing," but you can gather how communication is a blessing to the other person in something like this. Even better, if there's something specific you already know you want to work on, invite and bless people around you to inform you when you get it right and when you miss the mark.

The third element is perfection. While perfection is often not attainable, what I've learned is that when you're first embarking on any type of journey of change or transformation, you must be perfect (or nearly perfect) in your openness to the feedback. This can vary depending on the initial relationship trust levels, but you know well that if you bless someone to give you honest feedback and you're defensive the first time they offer it, they're unlikely to return to give you more in the future. As you build up the trust, you may be granted some grace when your response to feedback is less than open, but that's not likely early in the process.

While this process of blessing challengers is simple, it's also disruptive, especially in its vulnerability. In fact, if you're already thinking about people to bless as your challengers but feeling some resistance to certain people, that's probably the people you need to bless. Having "yes" people is not inviting challengers—it's asking people to tell you what you want to hear. There will always be risk (vulnerability) when you genuinely seek to get honest input and perspectives from people. This is just one of the many ways impactful leaders can and do model vulnerability.

# FINAL BLIND SPOT

I already alluded to the scenario where we start to believe that we've discovered all of our blind spots and this is perhaps the greatest blind spot of all. We all have blind spots and we'll all, ALWAYS, have blind spots because that's the nature of blind spots. Impactful and influential leadership is not pretending you don't have blind spots but instead embracing the truth that some blind spots are here to stay. Yes, if you're open and do the work, you'll identify blind spots and hopefully, take action to eliminate or reduce them. And that's when new blind spots—often more subtle and nuanced blind spots—come into existence.

For this reason, it's important to acknowledge the blind spot realities discussed above and to vulnerably and fully embrace the blind spot strategies above. This is all part of the process of shaking up your leadership, your self-perceptions and your leadership shifts on a path to continuous, ongoing growth and development as a person and a leader.

# Chapter 7

# Your Leadership Presence

YOU'VE HEARD IT said before, and you've likely said it yourself: "Wow, that person really has presence" or "I wish I had that kind of presence." However, have you ever really thought about what it is that you're labeling as presence? Have you considered the vital role that presence—being present—plays in leadership, relationships, trust and influence? Let's set the tone for this important chapter on presence with the summary conclusion from Amy Cuddy, author of the book *Presence: Bringing Your Boldest Self to Your Biggest Challenges* (2015): *the degree of your presence (experienced by others) is determined by your degree of presence (living in the state of presence).*

YES! People experience you as present when you're your most present. People feel seen, valued and heard when you give them the gift of your presence. Your presence and impact will amplify exponentially the deeper and more consistently you live in the present. The degree to which people trust you, engage with you, have your back and want to follow you is enhanced and accelerated by your presence. What an incredible return on Presence!

Even more important, being actually present for the people around you as a leader is a linchpin for impactful and influential leadership. In Chapter 5 (We've Got You), we emphasized the foundation of holistic safety in an organization and amongst a team. This includes the importance of the people around you feeling seen and heard, and they can only feel the experience of being seen, heard and valued when you consistently give them the gift of your presence.

While this may seem obvious, this simple yet challenging gift of presence is often denied to your people because you're "too busy" doing other things. Which brings up two questions/challenges:

1. *What are you too busy doing not to be present for and with your people? After all, leadership is about the people, and if you can't make time for your people, then where are you investing it? This is an example of leadership* gaps (see Chapter 6 for more on leadership gaps).

2. *What impact do you make on your people when you fail to make time for them and be present with them? Well, it's simple… they don't feel seen, heard or valued, which causes them to withhold their commitment, engagement, trust, innovation, collaboration and everything they have to offer.*

In short, when you're consistently and predictably present for and with your people, you receive everything you say you want from your people and team, thus enhancing your leadership. Likewise, when you fail to make time for and withhold your presence from your people, you fail to receive everything you say you want from your people and team. Are you getting the picture here in terms of the incredible value of your presence?

Given the obvious value of presence in leading your team, the challenge is not in understanding the importance of presence but navigating your way back to the present in order to receive the benefits of being present. You'll note that I said that this will be a journey back to presence. In the beginning—your beginning and my beginning—

we came into the world fully in the present at our births. I read some time ago that for unknown reasons, we're born with only two natural fears—the fear of falling (perhaps from being bounced around and carried in the womb hanging two feet off the ground) and the fear of loud noises. The rest of our fears are "gifted" to us through our life experiences and the people in our lives. Just as we're taught to be afraid, we're also taught not to be present.

When we're born, we only care about the present moment. We sleep when we're tired and we don't spend time thinking about it, we just do it. If we're hungry, we cry for food. It's not a thought process and we don't wonder if there will be enough food. We cry out and we get food. However, if there's no food, we unconsciously start to form beliefs about the existence of and access to food. Similarly, babies are not afraid. They might be startled, but they are not afraid because they don't know how to be. They have nothing to occupy their time with, hence, always living in the moment.

When we're born, we don't think about what happened yesterday or what might happen tomorrow and we don't think about what the people we're with are thinking about us. When a baby wets or soils its diaper, it doesn't get embarrassed and worry what others will think. It just did what it needed and wanted to do at the moment. All of this is to say that presence isn't something you search for and move toward, but rather something that you journey back to in order to live your life with a mindset and experience like that of a child.

Now that we've established that our path to the present is a journey back, it's time to start the journey of exploring what presence is and critically, what it's not.

## What's Presence?

Prior to reading Amy Cuddy's book, *Presence*, I had limited my commitment to and experience of presence to personal interactions—in other words, being fully present when I'm with other people. While this is a key element of presence, I took away a broader view of presence from Amy Cuddy and her book: "Presence manifests as confidence without arrogance (*Id.* at 34)." In what ways would your life and leadership be different if you were more consistently showing up with others in this form of presence? In what ways would your impact grow and accelerate if people most often experienced you as confident, enthusiastic, authentic and without arrogance?

One other thing to keep in mind about presence—it isn't necessarily an every moment thing. While I've made great strides in the quantity and depth of my presence, I have my moments when I'm not present. The question isn't whether you can achieve a 24 / 7 presence, but whether you're willing to do the work to put down your old ways in order to navigate toward living a life that is more in the present. To be clear, the journey back to the present never ends—it's a daily commitment and way of living that must be continually reaffirmed through awareness and practice.

With this foundation in mind, let's look at some clear examples of what it means to *not be present*:

- ❈ Having a conversation with someone while you're thinking about other things (e.g., your schedule, a project, your to-do list, an issue with another team member, etc.)
- ❈ Unwillingness to make eye contact with others
- ❈ Talking fast and being unwilling to pause or uncomfortable with taking a pause
- ❈ Engaging in a conversation and thinking about something that happened in the past (even if it was 10 minutes ago) or something you have to do in the future
- ❈ Listening to someone else speak while thinking about what you'll say in response

I could go on and on with examples, but the point is that when you're present, everything about you is here and now, allowing you to experience the moment. Critically, when you're present with someone, it's all about them—*when you're not present, you've allowed it to be all about you*. Therefore, committing to being present with others is a commitment to serving and servant leadership.

I could continue to share more about what presence is, however, I want you to know that presence is the most powerful state of being, both personally and professionally and certainly when it comes to leadership, trust and influence.

By now, you should be convinced that presence is THE answer and worth pursuing for your life and leadership journey. But if you're not, then here's what you must know: presence isn't only a gift, presence is THE GIFT. It's a gift you give yourself based on the differences it will make in your own life experience. How's that for a gift to yourself?

*Presence isn't only a gift, presence is THE GIFT.*

Even more important, presence is a gift that you give to everyone who experiences your presence. When you're present, you give another person the most powerful and loving gift there is to offer—the experience of being the most important person in the world at that *moment.* Are you ready to be the gift for yourself? Are you ready to give the gift of presence to others? Continue with me on this journey as we find our way back to the present.

## OBSTACLES TO PRESENCE

While the gifts of presence are clear, the journey to presence will have several obstacles to overcome and these two are the most daunting:

- Our culture today is designed for anything but presence, including the role of ready access to distracting technology.
- Your selfish nature will limit your presence.

While these obstacles are real, they can be overcome—sometimes slowly and in small steps, and sometimes in giant leaps of self-awareness. Every small step will help to accelerate your journey to a fuller and deeper presence.

The first obstacle to presence is based upon the habit of non-presence that you learned through the voices and actions of others from the moment you were born. While it's easy to blame our lack of presence on a distracted and distracting culture, the truth is that we've been creating a distracted culture and distracted personal interactions for decades. When were we most present? Before or after the invention of these now "old" technologies—the telephone, the radio and the television? While the cell phone and now smartphones moved us further away from presence, that habit had already been started by the various forms of technology available.

We also have been practicing non-present habits in our business dealings for decades. Think about where you sit when you're meeting someone in a restaurant or coffee shop. Are you facing the door where you can see everyone that comes in? Or are you willing to have your back to the door and focus on the person you're with? When you're out networking in business, are you fully focused on the person you're with, or are you keeping your eyes open to scan for other people you might see? What did you see practiced in your home when it came to being fully present and listening to others? Did your parents model presence and intentional listening? Or did they model distracted listening and perhaps hearing what's said in conversations without really investing in the person they were listening to? How long have you been told or shown that multi-tasking (not being present to one thing at a time) is the way to do and achieve more?

Essentially, most of us have been injected with non-presence for most of our existence, and thus getting back to presence will require that you put away old and deeply ingrained ways of thinking, living, communicating and relating.

Next, we come to perhaps the most obvious obstacle to presence today—our smartphones. How often do we see friends or family sitting together somewhere, and every person has their face buried in their phone? Perhaps this is your standard mode of interaction with others. Even if you think this isn't who you are, think again. I often hear people tell me how frustrated they are with people not being present, while they're some of the most non-present people I know. In other words, the absence of presence can be a huge blind spot for many of us. We're now so far removed from being present that presence has become uncomfortable. I regularly have people tell me that my presence—with my eyes, attention, intention, commitment and energy—is intense. We now have a culture where presence is considered foreign and uncomfortable. Talk about a significant obstacle to overcome!

Finally, we come to the obstacle of selfishness, which I'm guessing you'll reject as not true about you, but I hope you'll hang with me and be open to seeing the ways that our selfishness gets in the way of our presence. First, let's be clear on what it means to be selfish or self-focused—most fundamentally, it's simply whenever your focus is more on yourself. I'm not saying that this is always a bad thing but it can be an obstacle to presence.

Here are a number of examples of ways that we're selfish or overly self-focused that prevent us from being present:

* Sitting with someone in public while keeping your eye on who else is there so that you can say hello to them *is about you*

* "Listening" to someone talk while working on what you'll say in response *is about you*

* Keeping your eyes and ears open for the text or email on your phone *is about you*

* Talking over someone *is about you*

* Inserting yourself into someone else's story (e.g., when someone tells you a story about them, and you tell them about your "similar" story) *is about you*

* Monopolizing a conversation *is about you*

* Telling people what to do *is about you*

* Talking fast and not pausing *is about you*

* Convincing yourself that multi-tasking is more productive. Hence, your reason for multi-tasking when studies say otherwise *is about you*

Okay, enough … I'll stop there. Hopefully, you get the point. Here's a simple way to rephrase this concept—*if you want to be present for others, you have to make everything about others.* Unless and until you're willing to get yourself and your wants out of the way, you won't be able to give and receive this most amazing gift of presence. Yes, there are and always will be obstacles to presence, but they can be diminished and overcome, and the next section will give you tools for getting back to (and maintaining) your presence.

There's one other leadership tool that bears highlighting in this discussion of presence—the leadership superpower of silence. Most of us struggle with allowing silence, yet it's a vital tool for your leadership toolbox. Nearly all of us have the instinct to fill the space with words, which accelerates the pace of communication, encourages reactive communication and prevents the discomfort of silence from doing its work. Think about the meeting where you ask for input from others, and when you don't immediately get any, you quickly fill the space with more of your input—a lost opportunity. Likewise, consider the times when you ask for someone to take responsibility for a project and due to the lack of comfort with the silence, you or one of the usual suspects steps up to take it on. We also know that our need to offer solutions often ends up filling the silence when what was really needed by someone was to feel seen and heard.

Our discomfort with silence is yet another obstacle to presence and highlights the important need to slow down the pace of our leadership. While many leaders are obsessed with speeding up their leadership, more leaders need to slow down their leadership and busyness to enable them to be more thoughtful, discerning and observant. The pace of leadership has accelerated but at the cost of impactful and influential leadership. This aligns with my core philosophy that leaders don't run. There's very little in life that's life or mission-critical (and that requires running), but I've noticed over the years how I would often be literally running in my leadership. I realized that running is not my leadership—it's my doingship. If you're racing and filling the space, then you're likely in your own doingship. To empower your leadership, you must instead slow down and embrace silence as not only a leadership superpower but as a critical element of your presence.

For decades leadership has been thought to require someone who was willing and able to take up space with their ideas and words. In other words, leadership was believed to require filling up the space. Today, leaders must have the grounded confidence and inner peace to allow the space with silence, thereby allowing space for others to shine. Simply put, leadership is not about shining, but building, empowering and allowing your people to shine. Let's continue together on the journey to the present.

# GETTING PRESENT (AND STAYING THERE)

Ultimately, the best path back to the present is to move past the obstacles to the presence discussed above. However, we still need some tools to become present in the moment and then stay there. What follows are a couple of tangible tactics that will serve you well on your journey to the present, as well as a shift around commitments that will help you not only get present but stay present.

The first presence tool is the simplest, yet it requires you to be aware enough to know that you need to do it. All you need to do is take a breath. Yes, simply take a breath. I know you all think you take breaths every day, but the breathing you do all day is just surviving. You breathe and take breaths without thinking about it—it's automatic—but taking a purposeful and conscious breath requires that you slow down and often stop in the moment to take that breath. This works because in order to take a purposeful and intentional breath, you must be present, and the act of taking that breath is an action in the present moment. When you're taking a conscious breath, you're in the present. It really is that simple, yet deeply spiritual and profound.

Author and mindfulness thought leader, Thich Nhat Hanh, offers this regarding conscious breathing: "To take one mindful breath requires the presence of our mind, our body and our intention."[33] Indirectly connecting the dots between breathing and presence, Hanh goes on to write: "Thus, conscious breaths are a key element for finding your way back to the present."

The next presence tool can be done alone or in conjunction with the purposeful breath discussed above, and it requires that you do just one thing—ask yourself this question: *Am I present?* In order to ask yourself this question, you must be nearly present and when you ask yourself the question, you immediately become present. Even if you weren't present before the question, asking the question brings you immediately back to the present. You don't really even have to think about the answer because the mere question puts you in the present.

There you have it—two simple tools, a conscious breath and the question, "Am I present?," that are guaranteed to bring you to the present. Now the trick is to find a way to stay there for more than just that minor moment. The answer is really no trick at all but rather a commitment you can make both generally and in each moment, to every person you're interacting with.

The first step of the presence commitment is to make a global commitment to be present in every part of your life, whether it's in one-on-one interactions, group gatherings or when participating in a particular task or project. While a commitment alone will not ensure that you'll live and relate in the present, it will go a long way in orienting you toward presence. In addition, when you're committed to being present, it's much more difficult for distractions to take you out of the present. A big part of this is that your integrity is on the line once you make a commitment. In other words, when you're committed to being present, the internal drive of your integrity kicks into gear, helps you find your way to presence and keeps you there.

Let me be clear about the nature of this commitment to presence—it must be a real commitment. Vague statements you say to yourself or others, such as "I'd like to be more present" or "I wish I were more present," are not commitments. These are merely aspirations, and as such, they have very little impact on being more present. If they did, we'd all be living and leading more often in the present because there's certainly no shortage of people saying that they'd "like to be more present." Commitment means commitment—being clear with yourself and everyone around you that you're committed to being present. This opens the door to your enhanced presence and invites others around you to help you find the present and stay there.

If you've committed to others to be more present, also give them permission to tell you when they perceive that you're not being present. Knowing how difficult it often is for people to share difficult things with us, especially in the workplace, I suggest that you arm the people around you with a simple phrase to bring the question of presence to the table. In fact, a simple question is the answer when it comes to presence. Let everyone around you know that they're encouraged to ask you this question at any time: "Are you present?" As you already know from above, when you're asked this question by yourself or someone else, it immediately brings you to the present. It also allows you to be more aware of when you've not been present and to assess the obstacles to presence that you're experiencing. Other people can help you grow more into the present, but it first requires that you make an outward commitment to presence and ask to be held accountable for that commitment.

In addition to making a general commitment to presence, your journey to presence will be greatly enhanced and accelerated when you make specific presence commitments with the people around you. When you're about to have an interaction of any kind with someone, tell them (and thereby yourself as well) that you're committed to being present while you're together. Once you make such a commitment, it's much more difficult to fail to be present with them.

You can do the same thing in the moments when you're not able to be present but want to be present for someone in a future conversation or interaction. Take a look at this example:

Other Person:  Do you have a few minutes to talk about the project?

You:  Right now, I'm not able to be present with you, however, I want to be fully present for this conversation. Can we talk in thirty minutes, and I'll be present with you then?

Rather than pretending to be present or attempting to multi-task your way through the conversation, you stay present to whatever you're currently doing or working on (and thus are more productive). You also make a commitment to be present with and for this person when you have the later conversation as agreed. Thus, you set yourself up to be present with this person when you're together. You've now told yourself that you're committed to being present, and you've made the same commitment to them, for which they can hold you accountable.

There you have it—three simple tools to help you to live and lead in the present. First, take a conscious breath. Second, ask yourself the question, Am I present? Third, commit to being present, both generally and in particular interactions. When you infuse your life and leadership with these presence tools, you'll find that presence will become more and more your every day and every moment experience. As a result, you'll more often and more fully experience all the gifts of presence, which I'll walk through later in this chapter.

## Sharp Edges of Presence

Among the many challenges of living in the present, one difficulty is that it's so easy to wrongly believe that we're present and many of us have a false belief that we're more present than we actually are. The reality of the present is that it's a very sharp edge—you're either present or you're not present. You're not mostly present or sort of present—you are or are not. We also misunderstand the present, which keeps us from getting there, staying there and living there.

Despite the challenges of being present, presence itself is simple—it just means you're fully here, right now in this moment. This means that you're not thinking about other things, other places, other people or other to-dos. It means that you're fully with and attentive to whoever and whatever is before you, whether it's a person, task or project. It means that you're all in.

This doesn't mean that you don't have other thoughts, just that you're not allowing your thoughts to interfere with what or who is in front of you. For example, I often get ideas when I'm with someone else in a conversation. The act of having the idea (whether related to them or not) doesn't take me out of the present, but it quickly can if I allow myself to focus on that idea rather than the person or project in front of me. In order to stay present, I take a moment to jot down the idea for me to think about later. If I'm with someone at the time, I'll ask them for a brief moment to write the idea down, and I'll often tell them, "I want to write down this idea so that I can stay present with you." If I continue to think about the idea or try to make sure that I remember it, then I'm not present with the person I'm with.

You may not like it, but the present IS or is not. You're either in the present, or you're not. You're either present with the person you're with, or you're not. There are challenges to getting and staying present, but whether or not you're present is simple and clear. Now that you better understand the differences, my hope and desire is that you'll use this awareness to claim more presence in every part of your life. The gifts and rewards of presence are deep and profound, and they're all just around the corner.

# Presence Pillars (The Gifts)

It's long been talked about—gifts that keep on giving—but there's no greater or more impactful gift that *keeps on giving* than the gift of presence. Many of you have likely heard this phrase before—give the gift of presence—but do you really understand it and believe it? Perhaps even more important, the gift of presence has a unique aspect that no other gift provides. Presence is a gift that offers something both to the giver and the receiver. If I give someone else the gift of presence and live my life in the present, I receive a multitude of gifts—not from the other person or the world at large, but from and through the act of being present. In other words, presence is a two-way street by its very nature, making it the greatest gift. Let's now look at the many gifts of presence for the giver and the receiver—what I call the Presence Pillars. Once you know them, you'll want to make presence a part of every moment of your existence—not just because you're giving, but because you're ready to receive these incredible presence gifts for yourself.

Let's start with the most powerful gift element of presence, which is experienced by every person who receives your gift. When you care enough to be present, you send a powerful and empowering message to the other person or people. Even if it's typically unstated, being present for another person tells them that they're the most important person in that moment. More tangibly, the person who receives your full presence *feels* the truth that they're the most important person in that moment. This isn't an overstatement because the state of presence tells the other person that all that matters in that moment is them. According to Thich Nhat Hanh, "the most precious thing that you can offer your beloved is your presence."[34] Presence—an amazing gift indeed!

The people who receive your gift of presence may not be able to put words or even conscious thought to this, but the gift is received by them even if they're not aware of what exactly is happening. They'll also know that the gift you're giving them is unusual in today's culture. This also makes you unique in being one of the few people capable and committed enough to give this gift of presence.

The most empowering element of the gift of presence is that you get to decide which message you'll deliver. Will you give this gift of presence to others, or will you withhold it? Your gift of presence to others will pay huge and immediate dividends to yourself and your relationships in building, growing and accelerating trust. It's just the truth of the gift of presence.

## BE PRESENT NOW

Let's be honest—the path to the present is simple but challenging, and it represents a dramatic disruption of the status quo in the ways we typically interact with and engage (or not) with people. We've all been socialized and culturized away from the present and a multi-tasking and distracted existence has become the norm. In fact, our non-present state of "normal" will pull hard to keep you out of the present. The distractions will not cease simply because you desire to move more into the present, and you'll have to be fully committed to shake up your way of being and shake off your non-present ways of living.

And in case you're wondering where presence fits in this wide array of leadership shifts, presence is the foundation of it all. While the tools and shifts in this book will enhance and empower your leadership, presence is the secret sauce that will support and fuel all of them. Everything we've talked about to this point and everything yet to come is easier to achieve when you're in the present. Likewise, when you're in the present, you're in the best position and mindset to embrace and excel at all the leadership shifts and tools. Simply put, presence is the key to being the influential and impactful leader you most desire to be.

Now it's up to you. You have the presence awareness and the presence tools, and you also have the simple clarity about the gifts you give and receive when you're willing to be present. Presence is calling you—calling all of us. The present is waiting for you and your leadership. You may not have realized that you were so close, but now you see it. Now you know it. The only question is whether you'll trust it—and trust yourself—enough to take the leap into the present in order to give the people around you (the people you serve) the incredible gift of your presence. Now is the time, and the only question is up to you—will you leap, will you trust, will you commit and will you claim the present for yourself and everyone around you in your life and leadership?

# Chapter 8

# Walking the Talk in Leadership

BUSINESS BOOKS AND consultants all emphasize the importance of accountability, yet it's an often misunderstood and misinterpreted concept that must be clarified for the sake of leadership and organizations. This same sense of urgency applies to your own personal self-leadership, which has the most impact on what you do, how you do it and what you create. One of the most fundamental misconceptions about accountability is that it relates to getting people to do things. In other words, you tell people what they need to do or should do and *if / when they don't do it*, then you hold them accountable by delivering consequences. While consequences (of some form) may sometimes change behavior, the best way to sustainably change behavior and effectively execute is to model and support others to be self-accountable *even (and especially) when no one is watching.*

There are several critical elements needed in integrating accountability in business and culture. First, it's critical to clarify what it means to be accountable and debunk how we create easy-outs from accountability. Second, we must deepen our understanding of the elements of accountability and how impactful leaders model personal accountability and integrity. Indeed, our failure or unwillingness to equate lack of accountability with lack of integrity is one of the primary causes for our existing accountability crisis. When you embrace the reality that being out of accountability means that you're out of integrity, and therefore understand that choosing to honor your commitments (and thus be accountable) is the primary means for you to be in integrity, you'll find the motivation you need to do whatever it takes to stay in integrity. Another positive outcome is that you'll be more focused and intentional in making commitments, assessing your priorities and being clear about what it means to do whatever it takes.

> *Being out of accountability means that you're out of integrity.*

Imagine the impact if we created a culture of accountability and integrity. Talk about a game-changing shake up and shift in thinking and doing! This is precisely why self-accountability is such a core trait (and indeed a commitment itself) for impactful leaders.

## CLARIFYING ACCOUNTABILITY

Before we take a deeper dive into accountability, one foundational premise must be addressed: Accountability is ALWAYS a matter of self-accountability, not accountability to others. Lack of awareness and understanding about this fundamental truth is the most critical obstacle to becoming more accountable and creating greater accountability in your organization, team and personal life.

Yes, we often use the phrase that others will "hold us accountable," but the reality is that we're accountable to ourselves based on our commitments to others. I may make a commitment to someone else, but I'm accountable to myself. It's my integrity that's on the line when I make commitments. While others may deem me to lack integrity when I fail to honor commitments that I make, the issue is MY integrity. Therefore, accountability is always a matter of self-accountability. While other people can support me in being accountable, if I'm relying on other people to help me stay accountable by either doing it for me or taking on the responsibility to remind me, then I'm not fully committed and accountable.

For this reason, impactful leaders speak in terms of asking for support with commitments rather than abdicating the commitments and the accountability. Think about a common example of abdicating your personal accountability. You've made a commitment, but you ask someone else to remind you to do it. This certainly helps to make sure that you get it done and done on time because even if you forget, someone else will help you remember, however, who in this case is accountable? You made the commitment, but you're relying on someone else to remind you to do it. You've essentially asked another person to make a commitment to you so that you can honor your commitment. I'm NOT suggesting that you should be on your own in honoring your stated commitments, and you absolutely can and should seek out support from others, but the key question is whether you're getting support or abdicating responsibility for your own commitments.

If self-accountability is the opposite of blaming others, then what happens when you ask someone to help you stay accountable with your commitments? The answer is that you've created a situation where you can now blame someone else for your own failure to honor the commitment. This is the differentiator between accountable, impactful leaders and unaccountable, unimpactful leaders.

Similarly, if you actually need someone else to hold you accountable, then you're not really self-accountable. In my coaching work, part of my role is to provide accountability. The clients I work with make commitments to engage in certain specific activities over a certain period. The next time I meet or talk with them, I check in to see if they've honored their commitments. Many of my coaching clients admit, in the beginning, that they do the activities primarily because they don't want to admit to me that they didn't do what they committed to do. In other words, my check-ins motivate them to do what they said they'd do.

Do you see the problem with this model and thus the problem with any model that ultimately depends on people holding other people accountable? You guessed it—what happens when I'm no longer there to hold them accountable? The answer: They go back to the same behavior of not doing what they know they need to do and should do. While teams and organizations can create short-term accountability, if people have to hold other people accountable for long or even unlimited periods, this creates a heavy investment of time and manpower to achieve what should be achievable without this investment—people doing what they said they'd do and honoring their commitments. Holding others accountable also doesn't provide lasting results and is subject to failure at any time, especially when the person doing the "holding" isn't there to prevent the failure.

Organizations don't do well with accountability because they attempt to create an accountability culture based upon *holding others accountable* rather than based upon personal integrity and self-accountability. Instead of relying on other people to hold you accountable or help you remember to do what you said you'd do, try seeking support from others in being self-accountable (the impactful leader way).

Here's an example of the difference between getting help (abdicating) and getting support:

| | |
|---|---|
| Abdicating Accountability: | "Can *you* touch base with me on Thursday to make sure that I'm on track to have the report done by Monday at 5:00?" |
| Support for Self-Accountability: | "Can *I* touch base with you on Thursday to check in on my progress toward having the report done by Monday at 5:00 p.m.?" |

See the difference? Both demonstrate getting help with your commitment, but the first sets you up to blame someone else, while the second gives you support to stay in personal integrity by honoring your commitment. This is the way of an impactful leader.

One fundamental attribute of impactful leaders is that they walk the talk. Unlike leaders who talk a good game but walk a different one, impactful leaders make decisions, take action and show up in ways consistent with what they say they believe. The lack of congruence between a leader's words, beliefs and actions is at the heart of most of the disconnections and dysfunctions in organizations today. I often work with teams and organizations where the leader says that the team needs to be more accountable, yet when I meet with the team members, they're quick to tell me that the lack of accountability begins and ends with the leader. Why would a team change when their leaders aren't modeling what's being asked of the team? Answer: They won't. The team might pretend to go along with the change for a while, but they know things will go back to the way they were eventually because the leader isn't truly committed to any changes (because those changes would require the leader to change).

Are you prepared to do whatever it takes to honor your commitments? Are you prepared to be self-accountable in your life and as a leader? Follow me and we'll find out what it takes to claim and live this new way of leading.

Here's one more important clarification of accountability that's missed in many organizations and with many leaders. The fact that the organization typically meets external deadlines doesn't mean that the organization has a culture of accountability. Many businesses operate based upon external deadlines such as filing deadlines (legal and accounting), bid deadlines and legislative deadlines. While many businesses excel at meeting these external deadlines, I often find they're struggling with accountability internally. Several years ago, I met with a new team that I then worked with. As I started to discuss accountability, the CEO stopped me and went to great lengths to explain how well they did with accountability (citing examples of meeting external deadlines). I couldn't help but notice the many rolling eyes of the leadership team.

Later, when I met individually with each team member, I asked them about accountability and their responses were consistent—we do a terrible job with day-to-day accountability and the CEO is the worst at honoring their commitments. Yes, they met external deadlines, but the process was often chaotic, stressful and aggravating because of the lack of internal accountability. Thus, make sure that you don't confuse meeting external deadlines with internal accountability (people consistently and predictably doing what they say they'll do when they say they'll do it).

## THE ACCOUNTABILITY CRISIS

We're experiencing an accountability crisis and it's taking a heavy toll on individuals, families, relationships, communities, teams and organizations. Sadly, a promise no longer seems to mean much to most people. We make promises, we fail to honor them and it doesn't mean a thing. We don't care that we're not honoring promises and failing to do what we said we would do. To our individual and collective detriment, we say one thing and do another. We make promises and we fail without even giving our commitment the effort it requires.

Several years ago, I participated in a leadership program called *Whatever It Takes* (W.I.T.), the premise of which is simple: Make clear and action-oriented commitments *to yourself*, work with a small group to support you in your personal accountability and do *whatever it takes* to honor your commitments. In other words, it was an exercise to take my commitments seriously so that I wouldn't easily let them slip. The W.I.T. program gave me a whole new understanding of what it means to make a commitment and what it means to be self-accountable with *no excuses*.

I made commitments in three key areas of my life, including exercise. Like so many people, I know that exercise and nutrition are important to be healthy. Despite "knowing" the importance of exercise, I wasn't doing it and hadn't exercised much in the prior couple of years. One thing I liked about the W.I.T. program was that it was activities-focused rather than objectives-focused. In other words, while my physical goal included losing weight, my W.I.T. commitment was to do a certain amount of aerobic exercise every week (30 minutes of aerobic exercise—walking, running, biking or rowing—at least three times every week). Notice how specific my commitment was, with no room for fuzziness, gray areas or waffling. In fact, I measured my exercise time using a stopwatch to avoid the slippery outcome of saying that I exercised for "about" 30 minutes. Impactful leaders understand and embrace the importance of this level of commitment and clarity.

I was on target with all of my commitments through the first four weeks, but in the 5th week, I ran into a significant obstacle with my exercise commitment—pneumonia. While I could have continued to exercise with the pneumonia, I made a good choice not to exercise that week. Here is the interesting and critical point: I had a *really good reason* to justify not honoring my exercise commitments for that week. In fact, my W.I.T. group suggested that having pneumonia was a good enough reason to be able to say that I actually did meet my commitments, even though I chose not to exercise all week. I disagreed, and impactful leaders would certainly disagree.

Yes, I had a really good reason not to exercise, but the reality is that I still didn't honor my clear commitment. That's the thing about accountability—it's black and white. If you make (as you must) clear commitments, you either do it or you don't. There's no sort of, kind of or mostly and there's certainly no place for "I had a good reason" that I didn't honor my commitment. This black-and-white perspective is how impactful leaders view accountability; clear, concise and like the blade of a well-honed knife—in this case, the sharp edge of leadership.

Make no mistake, the clarity of a commitment doesn't mean that I will *always* honor the commitment. There are times that I knowingly choose not to honor a commitment or seek to modify a commitment. The key is that when I make changes with my commitments, I do so thoughtfully, purposefully and fully aware that I'm not honoring my commitment (rather than telling myself a story or not even giving it a thought). I'm also fully aware that not honoring a commitment will create impacts. We're all faced with conflicting commitments, however, if I'm more intentional in making my commitments, I will necessarily be more thoughtful to avoid conflicting commitments.

For example, recently, I had a telephone conference scheduled with a business associate. We had agreed to the date and time for the call, and I respected his time and knew that he was likely not to use that time for some other call or meeting. Therefore, I'm very hesitant to cancel any scheduled call or meeting. However, when it was time for the call, I was engaged in a deep and important conversation with my son, which dealt with a significant issue in his life. At that moment, I thoughtfully chose to reschedule my call to remain fully present with my son. I did fail to honor my scheduled call commitment, but I did so in full awareness that I was doing precisely that—not honoring a commitment and understanding that there might be impacts from that decision (even if unintended). I'm not suggesting that you'll never fail to honor a commitment, but if you're clear that you're making a commitment, you'll more consistently keep them *and* you'll only abandon or adjust them thoughtfully and with impact awareness.

Unfortunately, this type of what I consider "razor's edge accountability" is often lacking in our businesses, teams and personal lives. It would be good for all of us if a promise really meant something, but promises today often lack any real commitment, and people are all too often willing to *fail* to honor those promises. In my work with hundreds of teams, one theme is consistent—100 percent have listed lack of accountability as one of their top three challenges, and 80 percent of the time, lack of accountability is listed as the number one improvement opportunity. Number One! This further supports the reality that we have a significant accountability crisis in our culture and business world. Yet notably, accountability is something that you have direct control over because you have the opportunity to be personally accountable for your commitments.

In addition, you have the opportunity to help others be self-accountable. In my work with organizations, I found that the challenge isn't that accountability doesn't work (i.e., the organization practices holding team members accountable, but they don't comply). Rather, the organization, its team members and its leaders are doing a poor job of "holding" others accountable (or failing to do so completely), often stating that they don't know how to do it and that they can't hold someone else accountable that doesn't report to them. This belief is a fallacy. For now, it's enough to know that we're failing at accountability, and the key to changing this reality is to commit to and model self-accountability at a whole new level of personal integrity.

## Welcome Integrity

Think about how easy you say "yes" to a request. Did you think about it before you said "yes" and thereby made a promise? Did you ask any or all of these vital questions before you said "yes"?

* Do I have time available to honor this promise?
* What other priorities do I have that might impact or be impacted by this promise?
* Am I prepared to do whatever it takes to honor this promise?
* What other things am I saying "no" to in order to say "yes" to this thing?

The big question that overlays all such promises is this:

> Am I willing to put my personal integrity
> on the line to make this promise?

Most of us make promises without asking any of these questions, and thus we make promises without setting clear intentions to honor them. By definition, impactful leaders think through these similar questions so that they and the person to whom they're making the commitment are clear about the commitment and the accountability.

One differentiating trait of impactful leaders is that they understand the impact words have on behaviors, and one example of this understanding relates to the theme of *integrity* within accountability. I'd hope and expect that any promise would be treated as important by the person making it and that the person receiving it could count on it, yet that doesn't seem to be the case. Think about how often and how people easily (including you) agree to a demand, request or suggestion. Consider the following examples of exchanges that happen every day, both in the workplace and at home:

Question: Can you get this report to me by tomorrow?

Answer: Yes.

Question: Can you call the client today and check in with her?

Answer: Sure.

Question: I need a draft of this by Friday morning.

Answer: No problem.

Question: Do you have 15 minutes to talk about the issues with the customer?

Answer: Sure.

Question: Can you get the garage cleaned out this weekend?

Answer: Certainly.

Yes, these seem like fairly clear questions (setting of needs and expectations) with equally clear answers, however, they've come to mean much less than a commitment, and that's one reason our accountability has become so loose.

Here's where "integrity" comes in. The great thing about integrity is that it's something that people desire to be known for, something that other people want to see in a leader and something that we can control, mostly by becoming more purposeful about commitments, the meaning of integrity and the desire (demonstrated in actions) to be a person of integrity. Think about it, do you know anyone who wakes up in the morning and plans to be out of integrity during the day? Do you know anyone who has a daily goal to be out of integrity? Of course not.

I've discovered that most people want to be people of integrity, and even people who appear to be willing to not honor promises will change how they think and their behaviors by honoring their promises when they see the promises as commitments. They understand that not honoring commitments sets them up as lacking integrity. The problem is that culturally we let people (and ourselves) off the hook all the time when it comes to promises.

While it may be only a matter of a word (integrity), the impact is much bigger and it's transformational when it comes to accountability. If you treated every promise you make as a commitment (and ideally, you use the word *commitment*), then you'd do so knowing and understanding that if you fail to honor that commitment, then you're out of integrity. That's a big difference, and it impacts how often and in what ways you honor your commitments. It also impacts the degree of effort you'll invest to assure that you honor your commitments. If you knew that not honoring your commitment would create the reality of being out of integrity, how hard would you work to make sure you did what you said you'd do?

This is the way of impactful leaders and they take the extra step of incorporating that word ("integrity") when they fail to honor a commitment. Here's an example of how an impactful leader would take ownership and responsibility when they fail to meet a commitment: "I'm out of integrity. I committed to get this report to you by 5:00 p.m. on Friday, but I was late in getting the report to you."

While it may be difficult to fully tell the truth, this clear, intentional language of ownership changes everything for a self-accountable leader. It also proves itself as a powerful self-motivator to encourage people to be clear and purposeful in their commitments, do whatever it takes to honor those commitments and avoid being out of personal integrity.

When personal integrity is at stake, two things change: 1. People take their commitments more seriously in advance, knowing that their integrity is at risk if they fail to honor their commitments; 2. People are even more dedicated to the execution of their commitments in order to preserve their personal integrity.

## Clear Commitments

Just as the injection of the word *integrity* enhances the engagement of the person making the promise, making the word *commitment* a part of your accountability process further deepens that engagement. While it would be terrific if all our promises carried the same weight with us as our commitments, that's simply not the case. We swiftly agree or disagree to do things without considering the implications of those promises. Everything changes when we focus on *commitments*.

There are several key components of commitments:

* Use the term "commitment" with respect to your promises.
* Be clear in terms of exactly what you're committing to do (or not do).
* Be clear in terms of when or by when (timing) you'll do what you're committing to do.

Without this level of clarity, there can be no accountability. When we proceed with mere generalizations or vague promises, it's impossible to hold ourselves accountable and even more challenging to hold others accountable. This is why impactful leaders are invested in clarity of commitments.

I was recently invited to join the board of a non-profit organization. It was a great honor to be invited, but I had lots of questions before I gave my answer. I needed to know what they expected of me and know everything that's involved in being a board member. Without this information, I couldn't decide whether I was willing to make the commitment. Part of my intentional process of decision-making about commitments is that I typically don't make commitment decisions at that moment. When I make decisions at that moment, I tend to make decisions without considering my other short and long term priorities and commitments. This often results in unintended consequences such as conflicting or excessive commitments without enough time to honor them all. I also clarified that I needed a couple of days to consider their invitation and my response because I'd be fully engaged and committed if I made the commitment. In my words, I'd be IN! This whole process is part of being more intentional and impactful about my commitments.

When I work with teams and leaders, I often find that they're loose with their promises, vague with their commitments and unclear with setting expectations. When I ask people if they've set or given clear expectations, objectives and commitments, they often tell me that they've not been clear. For example, a typical question I ask the parties concerning a supposed promise / commitment is, "What exactly was the agreement?" I'm sure that you can guess what some typical answers would be:

* What agreement?
* What do you mean by the agreement?
* I'm not exactly sure.
* In general, it's ….
* My understanding was ….

Essentially, there was no clear agreement, no clear expectations and insufficient details and clarity to allow for any accountability, self or otherwise.

This is yet another example of a simple shift in accountability that can yield big rewards for everyone involved—understanding that we're entering into agreements when we make promises and commitments. I know this is probably a new concept to most of you, but the absence of this understanding impedes effective accountability for all. When you enter into agreements, you take them seriously. You think about what you're agreeing to, and you think about the consequences of your agreements. For more significant agreements, you may also seek outside input. Yet we often give little thought to what we're promising to do (or not do) and how those agreements impact other agreements that we've already made. Are you getting the picture? Are you starting to feel how elevating reactive promises to thoughtful agreements can change the likelihood of having those agreements honored and thereby keep us and others in more consistent and predictable accountability?

Think about the impact if you and everyone around you consistently do what you say you will do. Imagine the impact if everyone on your team or in your organization could reasonably expect that every person's promises / commitments would be honored. Much of our personal and organizational ineffectiveness results from lack of clarity in commitments and our inability to rely on each other in honoring our various commitments. Every time someone fails to do what they committed to, there's a likely snowball effect (short-term and long-term), the degree of which depends on the significance of the failure to meet expectations and how long it takes to get the commitment met:

- Execution is delayed (time that can't be recovered)
- Team members lose faith in each other
- Team members learn they can't trust each other
- Team members fail to support people that have already let them or the team down
- Projects lose momentum, stall or even fail
- Organizational objectives are delayed, miss opportunity windows or fail

On top of the foregoing, every delay in execution has a cost, and these additional costs can doom initiatives, projects and teams. The costs of ineffective execution (a clear failure of accountability) aren't just incremental, but they compound and build upon each other. Too many leaders believe that the missing link in their organization is execution, but the true missing link is accountability in most cases.

In summary, the following are the keys to enhancing your personal and organizational accountability, accelerating your personal and organizational effectiveness and delivering consistent and predictable outcomes:

- Integrate personal integrity and self-accountability into your organization
- Insist on clear expectations and commitments, by you and to you
- Consistently think in terms of making commitments, not just promises
- Treat your promises and those of others as agreements

These are hallmark traits and practices of impactful leaders and their organizations.

## Beware Covert Contracts

What's the answer most often given when people don't do what they said they'd do and fail to honor a promise? No, it's not to hold people accountable. It's not to support them in changing their behavior to honor promises in the future. It's not to help them understand the impact of their failure to honor their promise. Sadly, the most often given answer is, "Don't worry about it" or "That's okay." We let other people off the hook all the time because we struggle to know how to hold them accountable. We also struggle to hold people that don't report to us accountable. Many leaders also do this with themselves—let themselves off the hook—while impactful leaders treat every promise as a commitment by intentionally using the word *commitment* and holding themselves accountable with a razor-sharp edge.

After asking thousands of people this question—Why wouldn't I hold others accountable?—I found the resounding answer to be, "It allows me to be unaccountable." Yes, we often fail to hold others accountable and let them off the hook from their own commitments because we don't want to be held accountable (now or in the future). While the thought of letting others off the hook to justify my own lack of accountability may initially be confusing, it's highly logical and rational—and almost always done at an unconscious level. If I make it "okay" for you to miss a deadline or fail to honor a commitment, then it will be "okay" for me to do the same in the future. We often seek to avoid accountability to such a degree that we won't hold others accountable in order to create an environment where we don't have to be accountable.

This practice of letting others off the hook, believing that it will give you a free pass from your own commitments in the future, is called a *covert contract*. The "contract" is that *I won't hold you accountable if you won't hold me accountable*. It's covert because it's not conscious and the "parties" to the contract aren't really negotiating it or even having a conversation about it—it just plays out. Unless and until you admit the drivers of your own behavior, you can't change the behaviors. Only when you become more and more conscious of the drivers and thoughts that support your actions can you begin the process of shifting your thinking and owning your drivers, thereby allowing changes in your actions and behaviors.

If you doubt this current and prevalent act, think about your reaction when someone asks you to make a clear and time-sensitive commitment. Clarity causes resistance in us for two reasons. First, there's now a definitive time deadline for you to complete the task or project, and most of us don't like this definiteness. Second, this clarity of commitment now makes you subject to being held accountable, and most of us don't want to be subject to accountability. Remember the last time someone asked you for more clarity about a commitment. My guess is your response to a request for clarity—when you were asked to make a clear and accountable commitment—was that you got a little hesitant, uncomfortable or even resistant. This is the point where you might ask for time to think about it before making a clear commitment. This is what impactful leaders do—they don't make accountable commitments unless or until they've been able to consider their existing priorities and commitments so they can make the new commitment with integrity and with the full and *knowing* intention to honor the commitment. In contrast, the majority of our population today will simply agree, thereby making a loose promise without enough thought to be fully committed and accountable.

## THE ACCOUNTABILITY SHAKE UP

Yes, we have a cultural and business crisis with a lack of accountability. We don't understand accountability, are hesitant to make clear commitments and actually avoid making commitments to avoid being accountable. We're not doing the right things enough. We make promises without ever considering our other promises and priorities. We make promises and don't honor them. We rely on others to do what they say they'll do, but they come up short—and we say it's okay. We fail to do what we say we'll do, and it's okay. Are you getting the picture?

In contrast, snow globe leaders embrace self-accountability as a more authentic way of leading. While we're currently experiencing an accountability crisis, there's a simple solution to the crisis. It may not always be easy, but it's simple.

* Commit to personal integrity
* Be intentional with your commitments
* Make clear and specific commitments
* Embrace self-accountability with support

The time is now for this shift back to self-accountability.

As we discussed in Chapter 6, the greatest obstacle and blind spot to change is the false perception that we're better than we actually are. This blind spot is perhaps most prevalent when it comes to accountability in your organization and self-accountability for yourself. Keep this in mind as you assess yourself and your organization around accountability, and know that one of the biggest shake ups you may need to make is acknowledging that you're not as good as you think when it comes to accountability. It's up to you to choose to make the shifts in thinking and action to move yourself and your organization toward consistent and predictable self-accountability.

This is your crisis, and you have the opportunity to change things *for the better*. The shift to self-accountability is a shift that will make a difference in your leadership, and that shift happens as a result of small shifts in your thinking and actions. As an impactful leader, are you willing to clearly and unequivocally commit to this shift to becoming consistently and predictably accountable? This commitment level will, in turn, create an environment where your modeling of self-accountability will certainly support and empower others to make that same accountability commitment and shift.

# Chapter 9

# Actionizing Accountability

HAVING EXAMINED AND explored the key shakeups and shifts in our perceptions about and how we communicate about accountability, it's important that we also embrace a different approach to *doing* accountability. The nature of the conversations we have and our approach to them when we're out of account is part of the challenge we have in shifting our ways of accountability, whether it's someone else or yourself. While a shift in accountability mindset is essential, we must also shift the ways we engage and take action when accountability is an issue. This is where stickless accountability™ comes into play.

We're all too familiar with the carrot and the stick motivation theory, but it's time to lose the stick—in fact, to lose the carrot and the stick. "The carrot and the stick" theory revolves around motivating a mule—yes, a MULE! Thus, the theory begins askew because it treats team members as stubborn mules who will be motivated only by simple concepts of rewards or punishment. Frankly, this approach does a great disservice to our team members *and* ignores some basic flaws in the carrot and the stick theory itself. It also certainly fails the people-first culture test.

It's also true that punishment NEVER serves to build trust, engage team members or create a culture of safety. More importantly, the mere idea of using a "stick" is one of the key reasons why businesses struggle with holding people accountable. Since accountability is deemed the same as punishment, many businesses do a poor job of holding team members accountable.

To accelerate any business, we need a new, simple and effective approach to accountability. Welcome *Stickless Accountability*™ and it's three key elements:

* Crystal clarity of expectations (especially the what and the when)
* Clear ownership
* Simple and supportive accountability

Consistent application of these three ingredients will provide any organization with predictable and effective execution, resulting in organizational acceleration.

It sounds simple—***crystal clarity of expectations***—but the clarity of expectations is a big miss for most businesses for two reasons. First, most businesses assume they're already clear with expectations, making change unlikely since they think they're already doing it well. Second, they have a misguided view of what clarity is in terms of expectations. Here's a test: The next time you have a meeting, ask everyone to write down what was decided, who's responsible for it and when it will be completed. Like the old telephone game, you'll find that expectations are probably anything but clear. We live in a world where vagueness is acceptable (a great way to avoid being accountable), and we're so used to this vague approach that it takes heightened awareness and commitment to shift an organization into the realm where crystal clarity of expectations is the norm.

When it comes to this clarity, expectations must be defined regarding what's to be done or accomplished and when each part will be completed. Nearly everything that happens in a business is initially defined as a project, but breaking projects down into actionable parts or next actions is critical. Each next action should then be given definitive deadlines. This precision is essential to keeping projects on track and on time and to provide meaningful accountability check-ins throughout the process. Otherwise, we only know if we're on track at the end of the project when it's too late to make adjustments. Most of you will find your habits are built around project thinking and planning, and you'll need to be diligent in shifting over to an action plan approach to projects, commitments and accountability.

Even with the crystal clarity of expectations, adding the clear ownership ingredient into the mix is essential since ownership is another often-found gap. While many people may have responsibilities concerning a project or initiative, and many people may have ownership within the project, there can only be one person who has ultimate ownership of the desired outcome. This simplicity allows leadership and management to go to one person to determine a project's status and address any accountability issues. Yes, others will, in turn, be accountable to this one "owner" of the outcome, but the ultimate owner of an outcome must be clear in order to execute simple accountability. When the time comes for accountability, management must be able to go to one person, the owner of the outcome, to ask simple accountability questions.

## An Accountability Process

Finally, we come to the linchpin—***simple and supportive accountability!***
This form of accountability is NOT about punishment, consequences,
blame or shame. Instead, it's about supporting your team in an
environment of high expectations and continuous improvement.
The vast majority of people want to honor their commitments,
especially when the culture of a business makes it clear that honoring
commitments is a matter of personal integrity. Ask a room of 100
people if they want to be seen as persons of integrity, and you'll get
nearly 100% in agreement. Integrity is important for most people and
to maintain personal integrity, we must connect accountability with a
sense of maintaining personal integrity. When most people make clear
commitments, they'll do whatever it takes to honor those commitments
because they're "all in" with their own personal integrity.

With this backdrop of personal integrity, accountability can be
simple and massively effective—and it all happens with questions. In
Chapter 8, we addressed the need to assure what the agreement was
since, without a clear understanding of the agreement / commitment,
we can't have the accountability conversation. Assuming there's an
agreement on the commitment, here's how the process plays out:

> "Susan, you committed to completing a draft of the project
> plan by the end of the day on August 1st. Is it done?"

Susan can have only one of two answers: yes or no. If yes, then Susan
would be praised, congratulated and encouraged to continue her
impressive performance.

If her answer is no, this is where the accountable holding process
usually goes off course with a question like this:

> Why didn't you get the draft done on time?

In response, Susan will quite naturally unleash every conceivable excuse
for failing to honor her commitment.

This moment often makes me think of the scene in the movie 'The
Blues Brothers' when John Belushi's character (Jake Blues) is confronted
by Carrie Fisher's character (Mystery Woman) about missing their

wedding. I'm sure you'll remember that John Belushi unleashes his list of excuses with everything from "We ran out of gas" to "There was an earthquake." We laugh at this scene, but how different is this from our typical accountability conversations and excuses: I ran out of time; something came up; there was another emergency; I got another assignment; it was a busy week; I got busy. Sound and feel familiar?

The trouble with any version of "Why didn't you get this done?" is that it's effectively asking this question: "Can you please give me every possible excuse for not getting this done?" That's why you never want to ask such a question again.

The other typical failure in the accountability process is that we often follow up the team member's list of excuses with some ridiculous and unhelpful statements like, "Okay. Make sure you do better in the future." What? That's all we have to offer them—do better in the future? And in the future, what happens? The same thing—people say they'll do something, they don't, they make excuses and we tell them to do better. This is a failure of leadership, driven by a horrible approach and process, and the solution is the simple and supportive accountability process. Get ready to shake those accountability snow globes.

Once we've clarified the commitment and determined that it's not been met, here are the foundational questions of the simple and supportive accountability process:

1. What did you choose to do instead of honoring your commitment?

2. What's the impact of your failure to honor your commitment on others and the team?

3. What's the impact of your failure to honor your commitment on yourself?

4. In what ways can we support you in honoring your commitments in the future?

Notice that in this form of accountability, there's *never* a need for statements. You use only questions, all designed to help the *other person* see how their choices led to the failure to honor their commitment and the impact of those choices. The questions are also designed to help team members be able to consistently honor their commitments in the future—to do what they said they would do. Now let's explore each of the questions in this accountability process.

## CHOICES

I can pretty much assure you that when you first start using this process (including with yourself), the answer to the first question—"What did you choose to do instead?"—will be some version of "I didn't make any choices" or "Things just got away from me." The reason is simple—because this is the primary way we've been talking about accountability. We've typically created a practice and culture of excuses for accountability and commitments, so this approach will feel uncomfortable at the outset. Much like a new workout routine, focusing on choices will require a commitment to the process and helping people (starting with yourself) understand the many ways that our choices are the reason we get out of account.

Here's what you need to understand at the outset—identifying, owning and understanding the choices aspect is critical to changing our accountability approach and outcomes. Unless and until we're willing and able to "see" that our choices take us out of accountability, we'll be relegated to a culture of excuses, blame, victimhood and ongoing lack of accountability. This is where the influential leader must become skilled in the types of questions that will help their team members understand the choices that got in the way of honoring their commitments differently.

First, let's look at a couple of examples to help you understand the role of choices in accountability, and then we'll walk through some questions you can use to help your people understand choices differently. When I was participating in the Whatever It Takes program discussed in Chapter 8, one participant was an ocular surgeon, and he made a commitment to complete a certain project by Friday at 5:00 PM. When he checked in the following Monday, he admitted he hadn't honored the commitment. He'd blocked off time that Friday afternoon to complete the project, and he'd had a patient that required emergency eye surgery that Friday. Certainly, the eye surgery was a higher priority than the project, and he'd made the right decision to do the surgery. However, it's also true that he'd failed to honor his project commitment. This is the reality of commitment—we often have conflicting commitments that take us out of accountability, but there's still and always something to learn by understanding the simple accountability process.

When asked what he'd done instead of honoring the commitment, he kept insisting that he hadn't made any choices other than to do the emergency eye surgery. We collectively continued to ask him probing questions about any choices he'd made that set things up not to be able to honor the commitment, and that's when this awareness hit him—he'd put off the work on the project until Friday afternoon (right up against the deadline). As a result, he'd only be able to honor the commitment if nothing unexpected came up on Friday afternoon and we all know that the unexpected happens all the time. Thus, the unexpected is not really unexpected—it's simply unknown, and we can choose to make our plans around commitments knowing that some form of unexpected will happen.

Here's another more everyday example of choices impacting the failure to honor a commitment. Recently, I'd agreed to meet a client for a coaching session at a scheduled time, and I had a thirty (30) minute drive to his office. I had allowed some extra time in my departure to assure that I'd arrive on time, but right before I left the office, I *chose* to respond to an email that I told myself would only take a minute. In fact, it took closer to ten minutes, and while I still thought I'd make it on time, I ended up being a few minutes late for the client session. Obviously, what I chose to do instead of being on time was to take the risk of responding to the email (something that was important to me) rather than assuring that I left in time to meet the client (putting the client first).

Another typical choice that surfaces in these accountability conversations is not having a discussion about conflicting priorities. We often know we have conflicting project or task priorities, but we fail to choose to discuss this, especially when a commitment is requested. Certainly, someone's willingness to have this conversation, especially with someone more senior to them, raises issues of trust and organizational safety, but it's still a choice to have this conversation or not. These are the types of everyday conversations that can transform the accountability culture of a team and organization, and it's vital to clearly identify the choices that set up the ultimate lack of achievement of commitments and accountability issues.

Remember, identifying the choices is vital because only then do we help people actually do better and different in the future in honoring their commitments. Rather than just telling people to do better, we're helping them get better and be better in the future through this accountability process. And this is what leaders do—they help people grow and improve (not just tell them to do so).

## IMPACT

The next question in the simple accountability process is impact—impact on others and impact on the person who failed to honor their commitment. This is such a critical question and topic because it's the foundation of integrity-based accountability. It also allows you to determine if the person cares about being accountable and their intended and unintended impacts. Most importantly, we know that impact questions and answers will always get back to trust issues, which are key to shifting people's intentions, ownership and execution around commitments and self-accountability.

The answers to the first question—impact on others—is usually something like this:

* ❋ I made someone else's job more difficult or uncertain
* ❋ I created uncertainty or chaos for others
* ❋ I create additional stress on others
* ❋ I created a less than ideal outcome or experience for clients or customers
* ❋ I let team members down

And of course, I caused someone to trust me less or be unable to count on me. This is the power question and impact—trust—that typically drives people to be more consistently and predictably accountable.

The answers to the second question—impact on yourself—is usually a much shorter list and includes things like "I don't like this feeling,"

"I feel like I let people down," and "I feel bad about myself or my performance." This question is not intended to shame people, but to allow people to connect with how it feels not to be accountable. People who want to live and lead in integrity will be impacted by these feelings—people who don't care about integrity or accountability will self-identify, which sets you up to make clearer and quicker decisions about your team members.

The key to this question is to give someone the opportunity to self-assess and take personal ownership and responsibility for the impact of their lack of accountability. Rather than telling someone the impact, asking the questions and allowing them to answer the questions themselves transforms accountability from a fear-based, holding approach to a supportive, growth-oriented approach.

We'll talk more about impact in Chapter 11, but remember for now that these impact questions will have a transformational impact on your team members that care about their integrity and will allow your other team members to reveal themselves and their lack of accountability. This provides you with a clear path for assessing your team and making decisions about your team.

## SUPPORT AND ACCOUNTABILITY

This final question makes a real difference from other typical accountability approaches once you've gotten through the other questions in the simple accountability process:

> "In what ways can I / we support you to help assure that you're able to honor your commitments in the future?"

This question is the primary reason this simple accountability process is supportive and intended to change future outcomes, rather than punitive and intended as a gotcha.

Now, here's the catch—initially, many people will ask you to rescue them rather than support them. This is primarily because people don't have experience with support versus rescue. For example, at first, people are likely to ask you to support them by doing things *for them*—"Can you remind me of or check in with me about the deadline in the future?" In other words, people will often think that support means you helping them to stay accountable by putting things on your plate, which defeats the purpose of building a self-accountable culture. Don't fall for or into this trap.

Instead of doing things for others, support often means making yourself available. For example, while you wouldn't agree to remind them of the deadline or take the initiative to check in on them, you might offer support by saying, "No, I won't check in with you, but I'll make myself available for you to check in with me along the way." In the future, this person can ask for support in the form of access to check-ins, and you can mutually agree on a check-in schedule.

Another example of support that I often see team members request is, "It would be helpful to me if you'd be open to a conflicting priorities discussion when you ask me to take on something new." This establishes in advance an expectation that there'll be more communication about commitment and priorities in the future, making it more likely that commitments will be more thoughtfully made and more consistently achieved.

I've had some leaders ask me why they need to have these additional conversations, to which I ask this question:

> What's more important to you? Saving time and having the inconsistent achievement of commitments OR taking a little more time, having better communication and consistently relying on commitments being completed on time?

Notably, some leaders respond by saying that they shouldn't have to have these conversations and that people should simply get s**t done. You can probably guess two things: *how well they are at consistently honoring their own commitments and how well their teams do at accountability*.

Remember this truth—nearly all of us are less accountable than we think we are and will end up facing situations when it's nearly impossible to honor all of our commitments. Using this simple accountability process will not only make you and your team more consistently accountable, it also will help you achieve these **big four** for your team and organization:

1. More consistent and predictable execution
2. More consistent achievement of objectives including delivery on client and customer promises
3. Enhanced communication and expectations
4. Improved and growing trust and engagement throughout your organization and team

While some people may resort to blames and excuses, this supportive accountability model forces people instead to face and own their choices. What choices did they make that kept them from honoring their commitment! We also need to find out if they needed something else in terms of resources or support to honor their commitment. If so, they need to explain why they didn't seek what they needed before they failed to honor the commitment.

Notice that the entire process of accountability is based upon questions—no statements whatsoever—and is delivered in a supportive way to help people do a better job of honoring their commitments and being self-accountable. If the people on your team don't want to be accountable, then you have a bigger issue, and you probably have the wrong people on your team. It's that simple. There are plenty of good people who want to be accountable, especially if that accountability is designed to support and help them achieve their personal and organizational objectives.

Stickless accountability™ is mostly about setting clear expectations not only for what must be done (and by when) but also so that ownership of a project or outcome has real meaning (not necessarily just real consequences—i.e., the stick). Many people are uncomfortable when they're held accountable for their commitments, and this is healthy discomfort. I recently sat in on a team accountability meeting where a team member who hadn't done what he committed to do quickly and jokingly asked if the meeting could "move on." Why? Because being held accountable is uncomfortable, especially when you know with the simple accountability model that your failure to honor a commitment constitutes being out of integrity. The stick / punishment approach is about shame and belittling, but supportive accountability empowers team members to step into their personal integrity.

In case you're wondering, there's another disruptive bonus to *Stickless Accountability*™. It attracts and engages team members who want to be a part of an organization raising the bar and seeking to achieve great things. One of the biggest complaints I hear in organizations is from the people viewed as high achievers by the business. Their complaint is with the lack of accountability. They hate the idea that team members aren't required to make clear commitments. They hate the fact that team members are allowed to fail to execute without being held accountable. And they feel this way because the high performers almost always have their own high personal expectations, so they're often the most self-accountable. Even the high performers want to be held accountable for their commitments. Thus, a natural outcome of implementing *Stickless Accountability*™ is building a team of engaged and accountable high performers who ultimately become largely self-accountable. Of all the impactful outcomes that come from leading from a place of snow globe leadership, the transformation of people, processes and outcomes resulting from a culture of self-accountability is the most clear and measurable.

Imagine what embracing *Stickless Accountability*™ could mean for your organization—with crystal clarity of expectations, clear ownership and simple and supportive accountability. You would more consistently do the right things correctly and on time, thereby creating a model of predictable execution and ultimate acceleration, all while building an amazing team. What are you waiting for? Throw away the stick and the carrot and implement *Stickless Accountability*. You'll love the results!

# Chapter 10

# The Second Greatest Gift

IN CHAPTER 7, we talked about the greatest gift we can give or receive—the gift of another person's full presence—but there's another gift that's almost as great as the gift of presence. This gift is a critical factor in your growth as a leader and just as important, it's vital for you to fulfill your most important leadership responsibility of growing the people you serve. I'm talking about the gift of feedback. Despite feedback's important role in leadership, it's loaded with misconceptions, myths and misperceptions that we must shift away from for feedback to take its impactful place in your leadership growth and leadership toolkit.

How bad are our perceptions of what has become the "F" word of business, culture and leadership? A couple of years ago, I was speaking on this topic for a large group of human resource leaders, and a fellow HR consultant made this statement to me: "We might as well quit using the word 'feedback' because it's so tainted that it's unrecoverable." Wow—such a simple concept, yet we've screwed it up so badly that we may not even be able to continue using the word. Yes, I said "we" because we've all played a part in either tainting the concept of feedback or allowing feedback to get such a negative connotation. And because we've all played a role in its demise, we can all collectively and individually play a role in resurrecting, redefining and re-envisioning feedback so it can finally play the role it's meant to play in our leadership and personal growth.

To reinvigorate your leadership (your own and everyone around you), you must commit to and lean into this disruption in and around feedback. The stakes are high for your leadership and for every team member who wants and desires to grow, so grab your leadership snow globes and let's get shaking.

## The Trouble with Feedback

There are many obstacles to the necessary shifts around feedback, and there's one truth we can't ignore when it comes to feedback. A truth that will always be there no matter what other shifts we make regarding feedback. This truth is time—despite the many ways we can shift our feedback perspectives and practices, feedback conversations take some time, and that's why committing to feedback means prioritizing your time differently regarding feedback. Yes, there are many tools and strategies you can use to optimize the time you invest in feedback, but the investment of time will always be a key element of any shift in the quantity, quality and impact of feedback.

This reality prompted me to begin feedback discussions with leaders with this commitment exercise. I have the leaders take out a blank piece of paper and then ask them to write down the following commitment:

> "I always have time …. to ask questions, listen, provide timely feedback, care and serve. Always!"

Usually, they ask, "Now what?" when they finish writing. Then I invite them to sign it, and here comes the scary part, share it with their entire team. And yes, this is when the objections start flowing.

What's the first, sometimes only and biggest objection? Time. "I don't have time for this," "What if I don't have time for this," "I'm already struggling with time and other commitments." I also often get pushback in the form of something like I won't always have time, to which I respond: Yes, there will be times you don't have time *right now*, but if you regularly don't have time to give these gifts to your people then you're failing in your leadership responsibilities and opportunities.

In response, I ask them these four (4) questions:

1. Do you believe that it's important to make time for your people in this way?

2. Do you want to be a servant leader?

3. Do you agree that one of your key roles as a leader is to grow your people?

4. Are you committed to growing your leadership?

If their answer to any of these questions is "no," then we discuss what leadership means to them and what kind of leader they want to be. But if their answer to any of these questions (and hopefully to all four questions) is "yes," then they typically and immediately get it.

The truth is that your leadership growth is dependent on getting (and receiving) high quantity and quality feedback from others (see Chapter 6 on blind spots), and you can't fulfill your leadership responsibility to grow your people unless you're willing to provide the same to your team members consistently. Yes, time is a reality, and so is the importance of feedback, and it's up to you to make the decision—will you make the shifts that are required in order to be the leader you desire OR will you choose to abdicate your leadership by allowing time to be your excuse for failing to give the gift of feedback?

A significant shift required to enrich your feedback experience both as the giver and receiver is to dump one of our oldest ways of thinking about feedback—that feedback is calling someone out for the purpose of embarrassing them. Not only is it old school feedback thinking, but it's ineffective feedback and fails the basic test of helping people to grow and improve. We'll talk more about shifts away from old school feedback below, but for now, simply plant the seed that this type of feedback has no place in today's workplace or workforce.

One of the biggest shifts we need to make is to throw out the biggest misconception about feedback—that it's not personal. One of our favorite comments to others concerning feedback is some version of "Don't take this personally" or "Why are you taking this personally?" The misconception exists because feedback is, in fact, personal—in intent and impact. This doesn't mean that we should give feedback with an intention to hurt someone personally, but I've discovered over the years that the best feedback I've ever received stung—and it stung because it was true and because I was willing to "hear it" at a personal and then change-oriented way. In fact, if we don't allow ourselves to receive feedback and to hear it personally, then we simply dismiss it and move on.

I know your resistance is flaring right now because we've often referred to feedback as not being personal, but stick with me and let me prove (yes, prove) to you that feedback is intended to be personal. If you've ever given much feedback to someone else, I'm confident that you've more than once prefaced a piece of improvement feedback with this phrase: "Don't take this personally but [insert the feedback or criticism]." You likely meant it when you said it, but as we'll explore below, this preamble is for you, not for them. However, and here comes the proof, I'll wager that you've NEVER prefaced praise, a compliment or a blessing of someone's performance or for a job well done by saying, "Don't take this personally." The point is that we say we don't want people to take feedback personally only when it's about something they didn't do well or which they could have done better.

We would never praise someone and tell them not to take it personally. Why? Because we do want them to take feedback personally—all of it. If they don't take it, then they won't improve with it. This is one of the biggest challenges with feedback—we've been telling them not to take it personally for decades, which is another way of saying they shouldn't internalize it, learn from it and make changes based on it. No wonder feedback is failing so miserably and why so many leaders and organizations are ineffective when it comes to feedback.

Think about the most challenging improvement feedback you've ever received—the one that struck home. When we get high-quality improvement feedback, these moments can transform us going forward only if we're willing to hear and acknowledge its truth, and be personally committed to making the shifts to improve in the future. This is why feedback is indeed personal and why we must also address the misperceptions we have about feedback that make us tell people not to take it personally.

There are two more elements we need to discuss about the personal nature of feedback. First, the biggest driver for thinking that feedback is not personal and telling people not to take it personally is to protect ourselves. Unless you're a narcissist or sociopath, you have some level of desire to be liked (or at least to avoid being disliked). When someone says they don't care what people think of them, that makes me nervous because I know it's either not true or, if true, it doesn't bode well for the people who interact with them. While we desire to be liked at some level, we can still consistently deliver rich and growth-oriented feedback. Just be aware that when you're tempted to tell someone not to take your feedback personally, you're saying that to protect yourself (and the relationship) and that saying it may diminish the value and impact of the feedback.

Also, we have to differentiate feedback from what's often personally felt (not in a productive way) … the personal judgments about you or another person. One of the biggest challenges with feedback is that it's not actually feedback in terms of opinions, ideas and perspectives about the person's performance. Instead, it's a judgment about the person or a label put on their performance. Here are some unhelpful and often unhealthy types of judgmental feedback:

- ✳ "You really dropped the ball on this project."
- ✳ "You let down the team and me."
- ✳ "You're not working hard enough."
- ✳ "You're not working fast enough."
- ✳ "You need to speed up your work and make fewer mistakes."
- ✳ "You're careless."
- ✳ "You're a terrible manager."
- ✳ "You're failing as a manager."
- ✳ "You're not getting the job done."

While there may be facts to support any of these judgments, they're still judgments of the person, they don't offer anything to help the person learn, grow and improve, and it's lazy communication. To be clear, this is NOT feedback as we're discussing it and contemplating it for yourself and your team.

Think about how it feels to get feedback like this for yourself? Is it helpful? How does it make you feel? Does it motivate you to improve or make you afraid? Feedback is intended and designed to help people improve, and it's important to focus on the behaviors and mindsets that are getting in the way of people's performance accompanied by a sincere desire to help them improve. As I'll discuss below, the foregoing highlights why the best form of feedback is self-assessing questions rather than judgment-focused statements.

Before we move on from these key obstacles to impactful feedback, let's clarify two feedback truths. First, performance reviews are NOT feedback. Reviews (no matter how frequent) are a process designed as mile markers to assess how someone is performing relative to hopefully clearly communicated performance expectations. As you all know, performance reviews rarely offer any useful feedback other than the measurement against some standard, and the improvement opportunities are often stale, vague and already resolved. If you include performance reviews in your feedback discussions, you're mixing apples and oranges, and it's critical that you treat them as separate conversations. In fact, if you've built a rich culture of feedback, then the performance review process will be simplified and a mere confirmation of all the feedback the team member has received throughout the year or other review period.

Second, you must always remember that trust is the foundation of feedback. In other words, if you're having feedback challenges, then you also have trust challenges. It's a trust issue when you aren't open to feedback from others. If your people aren't open to helpful feedback, that's also a trust issue. If people are defensive when receiving feedback, it's a trust issue.

Think about it this way … if a team member trusts that the feedback they receive goes both ways (positive, reinforcing feedback and improvement focused feedback), is designed to help them grow and improve and is intended to help improve the team and organization, why would they ever be defensive? The problem is that they don't trust that the feedback is positively intended, the feedback is all negative or "constructive," and / or they don't trust the person giving it—often since the person giving it isn't open to feedback or is guilty of many of the same things they're giving feedback about. The bottom line is that robust cultures of feedback depend on trust and also build more trust, so make sure you're committed to trust (Chapter 3) as much as you're committed to feedback.

## THE TWO FACES OF FEEDBACK

When it comes to feedback, one thing is certain—we've forgotten in practice that feedback is both positive (praise, celebration, blessings, etc.) and constructive (focusing on misses and improvement opportunities). While we all nod our heads in acknowledgement that feedback includes both what you did well and what you need to improve, it's generally not the reality of delivering it to our team members (or even getting it for ourselves). When I ask the audience what they're expecting to hear when someone says, "I have some feedback for you," nearly everyone says they're expecting to hear about mistakes, things they need to improve, criticism, etc.

While we're on the word "criticism"—or as we like to dress it up, "constructive criticism"—it occurred to me a few years ago that even the word itself is harsh. Here's a test: try to smile while saying the word "criticism." You won't be able to do it because to say the word "criticism," you essentially have to scowl. No wonder we have massive issues with feedback.

Getting back to the two faces of feedback—positive and negative if we must label them—we know that feedback consists of both, but as woeful as our efforts are at constructive feedback, it's even more pathetic in terms of letting people know what they do well. The reasons are simple 1. Most of us were "trained" to focus on what's wrong and what needs improvement based on our prior experiences with feedback 2. It's easier to see the flaws or problems because they tend to stand out more. And when you combine these two reasons together (habit and instincts), you end up with a nasty cocktail that's big on what people did wrong and small on what they did right.

One other potential cause is that we fall into the trap of believing that getting it right is expected, and some people (pseudo leaders) believe that there's no reason to compliment or praise someone for doing what's expected of them. As a result, praise is reserved for those incredibly rare extraordinary successes despite the reality that it's the little rights that have the greatest impact on your overall performance and consistency of performance. In other words, highlighting and reinforcing the things people do well is the best and surest path to enhancing the overall team's and organization's performance, culture and engagement.

By the way, the consistent offering of high quantity, specific and high-quality praise is one of the key ingredients for building a culture of psychological safety (see Chapter 5). It's also been consistently shown that cultures that include high levels of praise and celebration score higher in engagement, trust, happiness, collaboration, innovation and everything else we say we desire from and for our teams and team members.

Before moving on to other key feedback shifts and strategies, this is the perfect place to highlight what I call the employee blessing. You don't have to call it a blessing, but in the example below, you'll see that there's something special about a blessing intention with your people. In simplest terms, a blessing has three (3) core elements:

1. Specificity—The praise is detailed and specific about the team member's actions

2. Small Ball—The praise is focused on small wins, successes and actions (not big wins)

3. Impact—The praise highlights the positive impacts of the team member's actions

One of the many positive impacts of a blessing is that it often helps the team members see more in themselves and their impact than they imagined. In other words, your blessing feedback helps someone better understand the value they bring to the organization and this is perhaps the best strategy to assure that your people feel seen, heard and valued—and to experience feeling like they matter.

During workshops and team sessions, I'll often ask for a team member to volunteer, and I then walk through something like this with them:

> **Jeff:** Are you open to feedback? (more on this concept— asking permission—later)

*Team Member:* Yes.

> **Jeff:** I wanted to let you know that I really appreciated the way you ran that meeting. You kept the team focused and on point, and I particularly liked the way you brought everyone back online when Joe and Susan went off on a tangent. Not only did you catch it quickly, you also addressed the distraction directly and in a good way which made the meeting more productive and modeled a better way to lead for the rest of the team, encouraging everyone to follow your lead. It also helped to build more trust by walking the talk regarding our commitment to more effective meetings. The way you led the meeting and kept us on track improves our meetings and makes us a better team and company. I want you to know that I see the ways you're stepping up in your leadership and having a positive impact here.

Let's check this against our big three:

1. Specific—Check
2. Small Ball—Check
3. Impact Focused—Check

What's sad is that when I lead this exercise at workshops, the person receiving the blessing often says that they've NEVER received that level of praise in their entire lives. In fact, the person usually gets emotional *even though it was just an exercise.* The bottom line is that your people are starving to be seen, acknowledged and celebrated, which is one of the core elements of impactful leaders. In case you're wondering, yes… in order to offer blessing feedback, you have to be more present and pay more attention to the ways your people are showing up and getting it right.

The question is not whether amping up your praise and blessings feedback will bring great value to the team and organization, but whether you're willing to invest just a small amount of additional attention, intention and time to gift this feedback to the people you lead.

## FEEDING THE HUNGER

Now that we've highlighted the key feedback obstacles and offered you several feedback shifts, let's explore some key tactical, strategic and mindset elements to amplify your feedback delivery and impact. Before we jump into these feedback fundamentals, let's clarify the apparent confusion around people's simultaneous desire for feedback and seeming reluctance to accept it. The simple truth is that most people (the best and right people) want to grow, and they know that feedback is critical for that growth. Another simple truth is that most people carry feedback baggage for all of the reasons discussed above (e.g., prior negative experiences around feedback such as lack of it, the harsh delivery of it and the nearly complete focus on criticism without much praise). In addition, trust issues (discussed above) have made people lean away from feedback rather than leaning into it.

The sum of all of this is that people want feedback, but they want it to be more helpful, more actionable, less judgmental and more genuinely given with a demonstrable desire to help them grow and develop. Thus, feedback is not the problem, but our feedback ways, means and mindsets are the problem. We'll talk more below about the many gifts of feedback but for now, let's shift to these feedback essentials:

* The best feedback is immediate and on the fly
* Great feedback requires greater leader attention, intention, awareness and presence
* Impactful feedback must be clear, fact focused and direct
* Encourage openness to feedback by asking permission
* The most important feedback tool is questions

## ON THE FLY

One of the biggest shortcomings of feedback is that it comes too late because it's delivered long after the events or actions that the feedback relates to. A classic example is saving the so-called feedback in the form of performance reviews, and as noted above, performance reviews are not feedback. However, many leaders and managers only offer "feedback" during a formal review process when the feedback is general and lacking in clarity, and nothing more than a judgment or observation. In addition, neither the person giving the feedback nor the person receiving it has enough clear memory to make the feedback or the receipt meaningful.

In addition, feedback is often delayed long enough so that the feedback conversation lacks details, context and clarity that would have made the feedback helpful. The truth about feedback is that it's best given immediately after the events that the feedback relates to and even a delay of a week or even a few days causes the richness of the feedback conversation to be lost. When the feedback is given on the fly or in the moment—immediately after the events or situation—it has the best opportunity to promote and fuel growth. The only exception is if the situation is emotionally charged by one or both people engaged in the conversation. In these situations, it's easy for the emotions to become the focus of the conversation and a short

*Feedback is best given immediately after the events that the feedback relates to.*

delay to diminish the emotional charge can be helpful. However, even if you allow a brief delay to allow the emotions to subside, it's still critical to give the feedback as quickly as possible so that both the giver and the receiver may have the freshest familiarity with all the layers of the events, actions and situation.

There are two reasons for these typical delays. The first is the mistaken idea that feedback conversations need to be scheduled and that they'll take a long time (which requires scheduling). As a result, these feedback conversations get put off while trying to "find the time," and with each passing hour or day, two things happen. One, the quality of the feedback goes down due to a lack of freshness from the time proximity to the events. Two, the resistance to the feedback conversations makes it more likely that the feedback conversation won't happen. And yes, resistance is the second reason for the typical delays. The person giving it is uncertain or hesitant (often for lack of confidence in the how and concerns about not being liked), and the person receiving it has built up resistance to feedback based on either prior experiences, the lack of feedback giving skills from this particular person or underlying trust or relationship issues with the giver of the feedback.

While all of these underlying sources of resistance must be addressed, keep in mind that the typical delays in having feedback conversations are one of the primary causes for the lack of quality feedback conversations. When it comes to feedback, the best mindset is just to do it NOW! Imagine you've come out of a meeting led by Sara, and immediately after the meeting, Sara's manager pulls her aside for a quality feedback conversation on what she did well, the positive impact of what she did well, what could be better in the future and the potential positive impacts of those improvements. Talk about a shift in approach and favorable impact. We'll talk more about a powerful feedback tool—the feedback loop—later in this chapter. For now, set an intention about the urgency of immediate and on-the-fly feedback. This one shift alone will immediately enhance your feedback conversations and the impact of those conversations for everyone, the team and the organization.

## High Attention, Awareness and Intention

To provide more high-quality feedback, paying more attention is one important shift to be considered. You must be more present with and around your people for you to clearly observe them and their performance, which allows you to enrich the quality and quantity of the feedback you're offering them. We talked about the importance of being more present in Chapter 7, and one of the additional benefits of greater presence is an improved quality of feedback. Simply put, if you want to consistently share and tell people around you what they're doing well and what they can improve, you have to pay more attention and be more present. In other words, to grow your feedback muscle, you must strengthen your presence muscle.

You must also amplify your intentionality around feedback, including your intention to commit to giving better feedback in order to help your people grow. You must also make a critical shift in the *why* behind your improved feedback. Feedback is often thought of as something that leaders and managers have to do (rather than want to do) and as a tool to improve the results for the business. But feedback is the most important tool for leaders and managers to fulfill their primary responsibility of growing and developing their people. In other words, to improve your feedback to others, you must embrace it as the caring thing to do as a leader.

If you really care about your people, you'll be willing to be more present and pay more attention so that you can give them the gift of feedback (praise and improvement opportunities). Basically, you must pay more attention to your people in order to provide them with the growth attention they need and desire in the form of helpful feedback.

## GET TO THE POINT

One of the biggest gaps in feedback is all the beating around the bush and preambling that causes the message to lack clarity and directness, especially with improvement feedback. At the end of the conversation, the person receiving the feedback is unclear what they can do to improve, or what the feedback means. Much of this results from our various resistance to giving feedback (see above), and the lack of clarity is often due to a lack of the presence, attention and intention discussed above.

Before continuing, let's make one thing clear about directness. In this context, I'm talking about keeping it simple and getting to the point—I'm NOT talking about genuinely harsh feedback that's more about personal judgments and delivered with anger or frustration. I often hear leaders say that people can't handle their feedback because they're "too direct," but this is rarely true. Their feedback failures are not due to being too direct but being too judgmental, emotional or unempathetic in giving their feedback.

Here are some classic examples of feedback that the giver feels are simply direct, and they can't understand why it's not received well:

- ❄ "You screwed up this project."
- ❄ "You're failing the team, the organization and me."
- ❄ "Your mistakes hurt the team."
- ❄ "I'm tired of you letting me down."
- ❄ "You have to get it together, or you won't be here."
- ❄ "You need to work faster and make fewer mistakes."

Sound familiar, whether you're used to hearing it or often deliver it?

Let's start by making one thing clear—the above and similar examples are NOT feedback as discussed in this chapter. Yes, it's words given under the guise of feedback, but they're not feedback. They're nothing more than opinions, judgments of the person, general comments and fear-based. They're not in any way designed to help someone learn, grow and improve.

Genuine and quality feedback can and must be direct (get to the point), clear and specific, and focused on impact and improvement opportunities. For example, rather than telling someone that they're making too many mistakes, identify the mistake, help them see the impact of their mistake, help them understand why the mistakes are made and offer them ideas to achieve the desired improvements. Clear, direct, non-judgmental and growth / improvement oriented.

## Ask Permission

One of the most impactful shifts I made in giving feedback is simple and designed to create greater openness to receiving the feedback. Like many leadership tools, it's founded on the simple ideas of invitation and respect. What has become routine for me, from intention and practice, is that I always ask for permission to give feedback using this simple question:

Are you open to feedback?

By genuinely asking this question, you show respect, treat the offered feedback as an invitation and open the person to receiving it by empowering them.

I use this question inside my team and often with clients and friends. I also make it clear with my team that while I do expect them to be open to feedback, they're fully empowered to say "not now."

There are many reasons someone might not be open to feedback right now. For example, their emotions or their perceptions of your emotions may make them hesitant to hear the feedback right now, and they may also know that they won't hear it well right now. There may also be other priorities, pressures or distractions that would keep them from being fully present for the feedback conversation right now. In these situations, accept their "not now" and make sure that you both commit to the conversations in a reasonable period of time.

The conversation might go like this, and notice there's no need to explain the reasons for the "not now:"

Manager:   Bob, are you open to feedback about how that meeting went?

Bob:   Not right now.

Manager:   Okay. Let's make sure we create some time for this conversation in the next 24 hours.

The point here is that asking permission to offer feedback offers so many benefits to the relationship, trust levels and the feedback conversations that it's an essential shift in your leadership.

## STOP TELLING AND START ASKING

In addition to all of the foregoing, the biggest shake up you can make in your approach to feedback conversations is to make them just that—a conversation—which means dumping statements and embracing questions. As we're all too familiar, most feedback is a one-sided conversation where the giver tells the receiver what they think, which is occasionally followed by a single question such as "What do you have to say about this?" or "Do you have anything to say?"

No wonder our past feedback practices have created such a dismal perspective on feedback.

Let's look at a simple example of the shift from telling feedback to questions-based feedback. Here's the statement-based feedback:

Manager: Your lack of attention to detail is slowing down this process for everyone.

Manager: It seems to me that you're getting distracted by other priorities, which has to stop.

Manager: Your lack of attention to detail is making everyone else's jobs more difficult and keeping us from meeting customer expectations. This has to improve immediately.

Manager: Let me tell you what I think you need to do.

Manager: What do you think?

Pretty typical approach to feedback, right? Lots of telling and no conversation at all.

Let's now look at a question-based approach to feedback:

Manager: How do you think you're doing with your performance with this process?

Manager: What do you think is causing these issues?

Manager: In what ways do you think this is impacting the rest of the team and our customers?

Manager: What are your ideas for addressing these issues?

It's a simple shift, but disruptive in impact and positive outcomes not only in the feedback conversation (which it truly is) and the likely improvements that will flow from the conversation.

One of the great benefits of questions-based feedback is that it invites the receiver of feedback to an empowered mindset of self-assessment and deeper ownership of both the praise-worthy performance and the improvement opportunities. Since feedback is largely irrelevant until embraced by the receiver, it's better to allow that ownership process from the start rather than hoping they'll choose to take ownership of your feedback statements and perspectives. As noted in Chapter 4 (Time to Get Naked), asking questions over making statements is a form of leadership vulnerability and this vulnerability will pay great returns in your approach to feedback.

Hopefully you've already embraced the power and empowerment of questions in feedback conversations and you're ready to dive right in with question-based feedback. If you really want to accelerate your feedback conversations, I offer you the feedback loop.

## THE FEEDBACK LOOP

The feedback loop is a process that will sometimes take additional time but its positive impact will reap you amazing returns on your time and intention invested. It's a way to bring all of the foregoing feedback improvements together in a single process designed to empower and accelerate growth and development, including your own if you're open to receiving feedback via a feedback loop.

As noted above, you'll notice that the feedback loop is a question-based approach and it's designed to nurture self-assessment, empowerment, a growth mindset, impact focus, praise and improvement opportunities. In short, it's the holy grail of feedback all packaged in a simple process and approach.

Here's the feedback process and the two (2) questions that are answered by both the receiver of feedback and the initiator of feedback:

❋ Feedback Initiator: What did you do well and why was it good?

    ✳ *Receiver answers the question sharing what they believe they did well and why it was good*

    ✳ *Giver answers the same question sharing what they believe the receiver did well and why it was good*

❋ Feedback Initiator: What would have been **even better** and why would it be better?

> ✳ *Receiver answers the question sharing what they believe they could have done even better and why that would be better*

> ✳ *Giver answers the same question sharing what they believe the receiver could have done even better and why that would be better*

Yes, it's that simple and even more powerful and impactful.

The feedback loop gives the receiver the opportunity to bless themselves by finding the good and sharing it. Please note that the receiver will often struggle with this initial question for two reasons. First, people have been taught to focus on their shortcomings. Second, most people are hesitant to talk about their positive performance. Don't let them skip past or rush this step, and you'll often hear someone respond by saying some version of "I did a few things well but let me tell you about the mistakes I made." DO NOT LET THEM miss this opportunity to highlight what they did well, and make sure that their response includes why it was good and / or created a positive impact or outcome.

As important as it is to highlight the positives, it's also important for learning and growth to be clear on why something is positive. This requires being clear about impacts. For example, saying that a certain action helps improve the team is too general. Drill down to focus on the ways that the action improves the team so that everyone is clear on the improvements, which will also identify other actions to make additional improvements.

Once the feedback receiver has shared what they did well and why it was good, it's important for the feedback initiator to offer *additional* examples of what the person did well and why it was good. This is where the presence, attention and intention discussed above is so vital—so that you can really see the ways your people are doing well and be ready to share them. Certainly you can confirm their own ideas on what they did well (and why), but identifying the many ways that your people get it right is a vital part of their growth and your leadership.

When we get to the improvement opportunities, notice the very specific language—*what would have been even better*. Not "what did you do wrong" or "what mistakes did you make." This is not about using kinder words, but about shifting the focus from doing wrong and making mistakes to finding improvement opportunities. After all, that's the purpose of feedback—to help people grow and improve—and the feedback loop brings together all the magic of rich feedback into a single process, all the while making personal growth and self-assessment the heart of the conversations. Not everyone on your team will embrace the feedback loop, but those who are committed to growth and improvement will embrace it and the rest will have revealed their lack of a growth mindset and commitment. What an amazing return on this simple process.

The feedback loop is a powerful leadership growth tool for you and your people. You may not use it in every situation but make it part of your regular feedback conversations and you'll immediately start to reap the benefits of improved communication, increased trust and accelerated growth and improvement.

## GIFTS OF FEEDBACK

Hopefully you already embrace the importance and critical role of feedback in growing your team, your business and your own leadership. Remember, feedback is vital for all of us to grow. As we leave the topic of feedback, I want to highlight what I call the gifts of feedback. Several years ago, I was speaking at a leadership conference in Athens, Greece and I asked the group what they see as the benefits of having a culture of rich feedback. Here's their list:

* Increased performance and people improvement
* Enhanced experience for everyone in the organization
* Improved outcomes
* Increased team motivation
* Greater transparency and improvement in trust
* Improved communication throughout the organization
* Clear message to the team that we "care about you and your future"

When I had captured their answers about the many benefits of feedback, I then asked them two questions:

1. Is there anything you do or could do in your organization that would deliver these returns? [The answer was no].

2. If these are the benefits of feedback, how do you not have time for feedback? [Silence]

Enough said!

Feedback is one of the greatest gifts we can give to another human being and it's certainly proven to be one of the greatest gifts I can receive, especially given the reality that I have and will always have blind spots. If I don't know it and see it, I can't improve it and the same is true for you and your people. Leadership is about helping your people see their brilliance, see the improvement opportunities and supporting them in achieving their desired growth and improvement. And feedback is THE tool for achieving this leadership impact. This may be uncomfortable at first, but if you embrace this shake up you'll find that you quickly and fundamentally disrupt your team, your performance, your trust levels and your leadership for more influence and impact.

# Chapter 11

# Impact Leadership

THROUGHOUT THIS BOOK, I've been sharing with you a wide range of shake-ups, shifts, disruptions, perspectives, strategies and tools to help you enhance your impact as a leader. However, there's one critical perspective shift that's required if you want to grow your leadership impact—you must embrace the truth that your leadership impact is significantly "impacted" (pun intended) by the degree to which you enhance your self-awareness of, intentionality about and commitment to the impact you have on others … especially unintended impact.

In the past few years, the following leadership truth has become crystal clear to me:

> Everything you do (or don't do) and everything you say (or don't say) has an impact, intended and unintended. Impactful leaders constantly scan for, consider and take responsibility for these unintended impacts.

This awareness and personal ownership of unintended impacts is a vital part of any leader's overall impact. Likewise, the inability or unwillingness to pay attention to and take ownership of these unintended impacts is one of the biggest leadership blind spots.

Too often, leaders want to be judged by their intentions and seek to be *off the hook* for any unintended impacts, and this creates a wide range of team gaps, including trust and safety. When a leader has a negative impact on the team or a team member and falls back to "I'm sorry" or "I didn't mean it that way," this disempowers team members and causes them to wonder about their value. When confronted with unintended impacts, how often have you said (or had someone else say to you), "I didn't mean it that way" or "I didn't intend it that way." Too often, our response to an identified unintended impact is to deflect and reject it as if impacts only matter if they're intended. Otherwise it's an oops, sorry and forget about it.

Think about how it feels when someone else says something like this to you, whether personally or professionally. Do you feel heard and valued OR do you feel unheard and devalued? Does your trust in that person go up OR does it go down? Are you more engaged and committed OR are you disengaged and less committed? For these reasons, a disruptive shift in your impact awareness, intention and ownership is critical in order to amplify your intended leadership impact and influence.

As we dive into the topic of impact awareness and responsibility, keep this wisdom in mind:

> "We judge ourselves based on our intentions, but we are judged by others based on our impact [intended and unintended]."

Clearly, impact is a critical element for any leader, which includes intended and unintended impacts. It would be great if our impact was limited to our intentions as leaders, but that's not the reality.

If you want to be an influential and impactful leader, it's vital that you take ownership of and responsibility for all of your impacts, whether you intended them or not. When leaders are conscious of, scan for and take ownership of all their impacts, team members will be more likely to follow, engage and commit. In short, your impact awareness will have a profound impact on your leadership and influence.

## UNINTENDED IMPACTS

This concept of unintended impacts was highlighted for me a few years ago when working with a business that had a significant issue with one team member. I'd talked to each team member, and I was asked to provide a quick overview of each person. I offered my thoughts on each person, highlighting my perceptions of their strengths and weaknesses, identifying hidden gems and noting areas of concern. My comments were balanced for each person except one team member (part of the administrative support team). When we got to her, my comment was, "Why is she still here?"

I went on to offer these four specific comments:

* She's clearly failing to meet expectations (and over a significant period of time)
* She's not open to feedback and was highly defensive about any feedback
* She neither expressed nor demonstrated any desire to improve
* Her attitude suggests a lack of care and concern for her performance, the team or the firm

All of this screamed time for a change, but the leaders were hesitant to fire her at that time because of the heavy work demands of the time of year. According to their rationalization, firing her at that time would put an unnecessary burden on the rest of the administrative team. They indicated a willingness to let her go once they got past this busy time, but they weren't willing to make a change now. I strongly encouraged them to make the change now, cautioning the risk of unintended consequences and impacts from the delay in firing her. But they stood by their decision to keep tolerating her (see Chapter 12) and decided to keep her.

After two months (the end of the busy season), they fired her for all the reasons cited at the outset, and they were looking forward to moving forward. However, they weren't prepared for what happened the following Monday after firing her on a Friday. Their top administrative team member quit—a shining star that the business was looking forward to being an important part of the future. Her primary reason for leaving—the failure to fire the underperforming person sooner. When pressed and after stating that they'd kept her on to relieve the burden on the rest of the team, the star team member offered this simple explanation:

> I'd have been happy to work extra to help pick up the slack if you'd fired her because I care about this place and the people here. However, by keeping her, I had to pick up her slack while you continued to pay her, which showed me that you didn't care about me or the rest of the team.

Hmmm … while claiming to be shocked at this unintended outcome, we can all see how this could be reasonably anticipated. As we'll walk through in more detail below, there's often a disconnect between our intended impact and message, and it's our unintended impacts and messages that hold back our leadership, impact, influence and culture.

Let's take a look at a handful of areas where leaders can have an unintended impact on and communicate an often-unintended message to their team members. One often seen example is leaders talking too much and not asking enough questions. When leaders insist on doing all the talking, having all the answers and mostly telling people what to do, there's an impact. This impact often involves a perceived message to your team members that their opinions (or they) don't matter, they're not important or they're incapable of independent ideas or decisions.

Another leadership gap is failure to be present and actually listen to your people (see Chapter 7). When leaders fail to listen or be present with their team members, the impact is often that team members don't feel heard or valued and tend to stay quiet and not speak up, and defer to the leader or other team members. This impact runs contrary to the goal of empowering and engaging your team.

As we discussed in the prior chapter, feedback is critical to grow, develop and engage your people. If leaders care about their team members and their growth and development, they'll commit to making the time and providing regular and specific feedback (praise and improvement). When leaders fail to make time to provide feedback to team members (or only provide critical feedback), the impact is that team members will feel they're always coming up short, will not trust the leader and will be hesitant to change and grow because they don't feel the leader is willing to invest in them.

One more basic leadership miss is in failing to "see" your team members. As we discussed in Chapter 5, team members want to feel seen and heard, which leads to a critical sense of value and safety. When leaders fail to "see" their team members, fail to catch them getting things right (positive feedback) and aren't willing to listen to them, team members will disengage, play it safe and refuse to engage with the leader, team and organization.

There are so many ways and times that we create unintended impacts, but few leaders make the commitment to be intentional about these impacts, as well as taking responsibility for and ownership of them. This impact blind spot keeps many leaders from achieving their desired outcomes and impact, and leads to many failures in achieving key leadership missions—empowerment, engagement, effectiveness and consistent execution.

## IMPACT INTENTION AND ATTENTION

One thing that's quite clear in leadership is an absence or shortage of attention to impact. Thus, the starting point for growing your impact awareness is to shift and enhance your impact intention. Clear proof of this gap comes whenever you ask yourself or someone else this simple question: "What was your intended impact?" Typically, the answer is some version of "I was focused on the intended outcome and I didn't think about the intended impact." While outcomes are important, the often-singular focus on outcomes without much attention to people-impact results in either unachieved outcomes or outcomes achieved at a high people and culture price.

As I've highlighted throughout this book, one of the leader's greatest impact tools is questions, and the shift to questions is essential to amplify your impact and influence. When it comes to impact awareness and ownership, I've developed this simple and transformational set of four (4) questions to use before and after you make any decision, take any action or engage in any communication.

1.   What is (or was) your intended impact?
2.   What is (or was) your intended message?
3.   What *might be (or have been)* the unintended impact?
4.   What *might be (or have been)* the unintended message?

With full pun intended, the foundation of all of these questions is to be more intentional in enhancing intended impact and minimizing unintended impact.

Before sharing a couple of illustrative examples, let's focus on the difference between impact and message. While impact can seem like an outcome, it's typically broader in scope and purpose. In addition, outcomes are more linear while impact is more about deeper and longer-term ripples. For example, you may make a decision in the hopes of achieving a particular business goal but the desired and intended impact would likely go behind the specific goal.

The difference between impact and message refers to the message you hope to communicate—not the specific words but the overall understanding of the receiver—through the action, decision or communication. For example, your intended impact of a decision might be to motivate the team to work together, and your intended message might be that collaboration is a core value in the organization. In practice, not enough intention is given to either the intended impact or message, as evidenced by the blank stares I usually get when I ask a leader one of these questions:

What's your intended impact?

*What was your intended impact?*

What's your intended message?

*What was your intended message?*

Simply put, we're typically not intentional about impact and we almost never think about the message. Taking the time and attention to consider these questions in advance, and to assess them after the fact, is a critical foundation in shaking up and shifting your leadership impact and influence.

Let's use these questions to assess the scenario above with the non-performing team member and the decision to delay firing her. The first question—What's the intended impact of delaying the firing of the team member?—could be considered in terms of the impact on the employee, the team and the organization. Let's consider all three:

* Intended impact on the non-performing team member—*You might think the intended impact was to give her a chance to improve, but everyone agreed that she wasn't likely to improve.*

* Intended impact on the team—*To avoid putting an extraordinary burden on the rest of the team during a busy time.*

* Intended impact on the organization—*To assure that the organization had a full team (even if underperforming) during a busy time and heavy client demands.*

In this case, these intentions were considered and discussed. Now let's look at the message questions:

* Intended message to the non-performing team member—*The only possible message to the team member is that she would continue to get a chance to improve, but the leaders were not really committed to that chance.*

* Intended message to the team—*We care about you and don't want to overwork you.*

* Intended message to the organization—*We give our people many chances to perform and want you to succeed.*

If you're already struggling with whether these intended messages make sense or are likely to be "heard," then you're ahead of the game in your leadership. You probably also won't be surprised at the unintended impacts and messages.

As for the potential unintended impacts and messages of the decision to keep the employee on through the busy time, there wasn't a great deal of attention given to it other than a general conversation that the rest of the team was already frustrated by the underperforming team member and what appeared to be a lack of concern or attention from the organization. In the rearview mirror, however, we can accurately assess the unintended impacts and messages. Note the slight difference in the questions here—*what might have been*—since we won't always know the unintended impact and messages.

- Unintended impact on the non-performing team member— *She likely believed that her job was more secure than it was and her termination may have come as a surprise. [Hint: If you're leading, managing and communicating well, people will never be surprised when they're fired.]*

- Unintended impact to the team—*Their best performing and most committed team member quit and there were likely additional unintended impacts with the rest of the team from the original decision and certainly when their best team member quit.*

- Unintended impact on the organization—*Other team members believe that performance expectations don't mean anything, and a lack of accountability becomes the culture of the organization.*

Paraphrasing Batman, "Holy Impact!" Just imagine the cost of these unintended impacts to people, performance and culture.

Similarly, the rearview mirror allows us to consider the actual and potential unintended messages from this decision.

- Unintended message to the non-performing team member— *You're an important part of this team and we're committed to your success.*

- Unintended messages to the team—*We don't care about you and we're willing to make you work harder to cover up for an underperforming employee. We aren't willing to make the hard decisions and you'll pay the price.*

- Unintended message to the organization—*We don't care if you perform or support the team. All you have to do is show up and that's enough.*

Again, imagine the albeit unintended ripples that this one decision had throughout the organization. This doesn't mean that we won't make mistakes as leaders, but the essential starting point is to be more intentional about your intentions and commit yourself to more thoughtfully assessing the potential or actual unintended impacts and messages that flow from your decisions, non-decisions, actions, inaction, communication and lack of communication.

If you're feeling the bar raise on leadership—your leadership— you're right and that's the nature of leadership. Leadership is not for everyone, but it's open to everyone and embracing this impact mindset and process in your leadership is proof of your personal commitment to step up and shake up your leadership impact and influence.

One final thought before we move on to a couple more impact essentials. One of the keys to everything discussed above is that the approach and process helps our people to see their impact, which is one vital function of leaders. It's your responsibility to help your people see their impact, intended and unintended, and help them start to see around those corners (even everyday corners) to maximize their intended impacts and minimize their unintended impacts. And if you're going to help your people see it, you must first be willing to vulnerably embark on your own journey of increased and intentional impact awareness and ownership.

I alluded to it above and it can't be overstated—we're not perfect, which means we'll inevitably and sometimes more often than we'd like, create unintended impacts. The question is not whether we'll all be the orchestrators of unintended impacts (even if unconsciously) but in what ways we respond when we do. Will you react, defend and deny or will you pause, reflect and take ownership? Leadership is about vulnerably taking personal responsibility for the impacts you create, especially unintended impacts.

Too often, our response is to abdicate and deflect by hiding behind our lack of intention, thereby hoping to negate the reality of our impact. People are tired of hearing leaders avoid responsibility by relying on a lack of intent around their impact. People are looking for leaders they can trust to take responsibility and ownership for their impacts, both intended and unintended. This is another of the foundations for the concept discussed in Chapter 3, that leaders don't apologize but instead take responsibility, seek to learn and commit to minimizing their unintended impacts in the future.

If you're committed to minimizing your unintended impacts and messages and maximizing your personal responsibility and ownership of those impacts and messages, then you'll need to lean on another empowering leadership tool—the leader pause.

## THE LEADER PAUSE

Now that you've committed to grow your leadership around impact intention, awareness and responsibility, you must enhance your ability to create space for this intention, awareness and responsibility. The leader pause is your solution.

I recently had an unexpected encounter with one of the audience members in a large group setting where I was speaking. I couldn't read her name tag and I didn't hear her (due to my hearing loss) when I asked for her name. As a result, I mispronounced her name. I quickly apologized and went on with my hypothetical question to her, which concluded with "what would you think?" Her response caught me off guard as she ignored my actual question and sarcastically said, "I'd think you don't know my name." I thought she was making a joke, but then I realized that she was actually upset. Clearly, my mispronunciation of her name had impacted her and she was directing that impact back at me.

Honestly, I was angered by her response—mainly because I'd pronounced her name wrong because I legitimately couldn't hear her due to my hearing issues, which I had told her. I was angry because I felt like she was attacking me because I couldn't hear her, and my hearing loss bothers me. In short, I was triggered by her response, and I wanted to fire something back at her. Instead, and in the moment (literally just an instant), I processed all of the foregoing information, including my anger, the triggering and the core of the triggering (my self-consciousness about my hearing loss). Instead of firing back at her, I calmly continued with her and got back on track with my questions and the program.

You might be thinking that I merely resisted the urge to fire back at her due to the circumstances, but you'd be wrong. The truth is that I processed everything at that moment and in doing so, my anger was gone. I fully understood what had triggered me, and I could communicate with her without the anger, without sarcasm and without even subtly firing back. Why? It was all because of *the leader pause.*

Over the past years, I've discovered the power and impact of the leader pause, a tool that leaders must develop to be their most effective at communicating, building relationships and fostering trust. The leader pause is the momentary pause where a leader does all the things that make leaders most impactful:

* Thinks about and is conscious of their intended impact and potential unintended impact
* Catches themselves getting triggered
* Processes their emotions and energy in order to communicate without the energy that impedes good communication
* Processes what they've just heard from someone else or in a meeting *before* responding
* Makes time to listen to, hear and really see their team members even amid a full schedule and pressing priorities
* Remains present in any interaction

Many leaders know what to do (or what not to do), but they get caught up in the fast pace of business, communication and human interactions, so they forget to do what they already know. In many cases, this is some form of a reaction versus a thoughtful action, and the shift to thoughtful action is all about the leader pause.

Think about it: all the times and situations, whether personally or professionally, where you would have done something differently (or not done something) if you'd only been able to pause for a moment. When your team member comes to you with a question but you're focused on something else, and you dismiss them. When your partner wants to share something with you but you're focused on work and you aren't present for them. When your children ask you to play with them and you quickly tell them that you're too busy right now. In some cases, your choices might not change, but they'll still be more conscious and thoughtful when you find and practice the leader pause.

The leader pause is much like what high-performing athletes talk about when they say that everything seems to slow down despite the rapid pace of the game. When an athlete is in the zone, they process massive amounts of information and choices instantly while making good decisions. In other words, the game is speeding up but they're slowing down in the midst of the speed of the game. That's the essence of the leader pause.

Your ability to find and practice the leader pause will somewhat depend on experience, but there are a few elements that you can practice and hone:

* First, look for the leader pause. When you look for it, you're more likely to find it and practice it.

* Second, breathe. You heard me—breathe. When you consciously take a breath, you create space for the pause.

* Third, commit to the pause. The more intentional you are about the importance of the pause, the more likely you are to find it and make space for it.

* Fourth, use this simple question to create space for the pause—ask yourself, "Am I present?" When you ask this question, you automatically get present and the pause exists in that presence.

* Finally, regularly review and assess your communication and relational interactions (even after the fact) to learn more about yourself and your reactions. It may be after the fact, but the better you understand yourself, the better you'll be able to navigate future interactions and situations using the pause.

This shift to the leader pause may be difficult, but it's a simple concept. It's up to you whether you care enough about your leadership and the people your leadership impacts to commit to embracing and honing your leader pause.

If you're wondering about the why behind the leader pause, it's simple—better relationships, deeper trust, more influence and impact and more effective communication. Not bad for just a pause—*The Leader Pause.*

# Disrupting Your Disruption

It's quite the paradox—your lack of attention to, intention about and awareness of your unintended impacts and messages creates a great deal of unintended and undesired outcomes and experiences, especially for the people around you. At the same time, disruption in your thinking, mindset and approach to impacts is vital in order to diminish the impact disruption you're already creating. This is precisely the concept behind snow globe leadership—disrupting your thinking, perceptions and actions in order to disrupt your leadership and empower your intended impact and influence.

Let's face it—it's always easier to deflect, defend and deny when it comes to unintended impacts and messages. And it's uncomfortable to assess, own and adjust to minimize those same unintended impacts and messages. At this inflexion point of necessary discomfort lies one of your foundational leadership edges and decision points. Will you choose to hope to be judged based on your good intentions or will you choose to take responsibility for all of your impacts, intended and unintended, instead?

Of all the topics discussed in this book, the lack and often absence of impact awareness, intention and ownership in leadership is perhaps the most damaging and limiting in terms of your desired outcomes and objectives. Leadership is about people and the ways you impact those people matters more than anything you do in your leadership. This is a call to shake up your leadership in order to not only address the people-challenges of our time but build the trust, engagement and culture that will serve your people and your mission. Will you answer the shake up call or leave your leadership on the shelf to settle and fade away?

# Chapter 12

# The Tolerance Factor

IF YOU HAVEN'T already figured it out, I love shaking things up—people, thinking, perspectives and leadership—which means that I also love sharing disruptive ideas for people and leaders. There's no coincidence that this is almost the final chapter of leadership shifts and tools because it's been the most disruptive concept I've shared over the past years. In fact, the very first time I shared this concept with a group of business owners, an attendee jumped out of their chair and shouted, "That's not true." That's when I knew I'd discovered something that had the potential to shake up leaders, teams, organizations, cultures and outcomes in transformational ways.

Here's what I shared a few years ago when speaking at a conference in Las Vegas:

> "Your leadership, culture and impact are
> not defined by what you preach,
> ***but by what and who you tolerate.***"

Yes, your tolerance is the most impactful element of your leadership, culture and outcomes, and it's often (if not nearly always) ignored at great peril and negative impact.

A few years ago, when I shared this simple concept that evoked a strong reaction from the one attendee, I embraced the challenge and asked the attendee, "What about this isn't true?" In response, he indicated that he was tolerating someone in his organization but had good reasons for doing so. The following is an overview of the exchange that followed:

| | |
|---|---|
| Me: | What exactly have you been tolerating? |
| Attendee: | I have a business partner that can be pretty verbally brutal. He can be a bit of an a\*\*hole. |
| Me: | What's your excuse for tolerating this partner? |
| Attendee: | It's not an excuse. It's a reason. |
| Me: | Do you know the difference between an excuse and a reason? An excuse feels better. |
| Attendee: | [Lowering his head a bit] … He brings in a lot of business, and he's my brother. |
| Me: | So, your risk is Thanksgiving dinner. What do you think the impact of tolerating this abusive partner is on your team? |
| Attendee: | I know they don't enjoy it when he acts this way and they may think that I don't care about them because I allow it to continue. |
| Me: | And what might be the message that your team "hears" from you tolerating this abusive partner? |
| Attendee: | Perhaps that I don't care about them and that I think the verbal abuse is okay. |

Hopefully you're getting the point, and this is the reality of tolerance— *what and who we tolerate becomes the truth of the culture and organization (rather than the exception)*. We all want to believe that we can have certain values and a particular culture while allowing some exceptions, but **the truth is that those exceptions define the values and culture.**

This is the foundation of tolerance and what I refer to as your tolerance factor, and your tolerance factor will define your leadership, culture and impact (or lack thereof).

## Your Tolerance Factor

Let's make one thing clear at the outset—the tolerance I'm discussing refers to people, behavior and actions that are outside your stated values and expectations. This isn't about the vital need to amplify our tolerance levels regarding differences (cultural, racial, gender, etc.). While building more diverse, equitable and inclusive teams and organizations is critical, that's a topic for another book. I do want to be clear that this discussion of tolerance and tolerance factors is NOT about diminishing tolerance of differences. Building more diverse and inclusive cultures of belonging is essential, and the tolerance discussed in this chapter is an entirely different conversation. In fact, your limiting tolerance factor may include diversity, equity and inclusion issues and tolerances.

As we begin this journey into tolerance and your tolerance factor, ask yourself this question: **What or who are you tolerating?** Whether it's in your organization, within your team, in your leadership, with those you serve, in your personal life or your relationships, what behavior or situations, and what people are you tolerating? It's important to honestly assess WHY you're tolerating the people, situations or behavior. As noted in the example above, perhaps the tolerance is relationship-based, and you're hesitant to set and hold expectations and boundaries for fear of impacting relationships. Also, as above, maybe the tolerance is based upon some level or unique nature of value that you perceive to be delivered by the people associated with the tolerance.

We've all seen this situation before—a perceived high performer is allowed to engage in behavior that's otherwise not acceptable or allowed to ignore processes and procedures that are enforced with everyone else. Another rampant form of tolerance is allowing underperformers to continue underperforming without efforts to improve them or exit them from the organization. One question I typically ask people when I start working with an organization is, "How hard or easy is it to get fired here?" Most often, the answer is that it's incredibly difficult to get fired and not in a good way. The funniest response I ever heard was, "You'd have to kill someone that everyone likes to get fired." Let's face it, while we want everyone to succeed, continuing to allow people to underperform without improvement or without removing them is one of the most common and culture-killing forms of tolerance.

Another common tolerance area is having different standards for people, especially as it relates to policies and procedures. When you have different standards without reason, people lose trust and choose not to engage. When your words and actions are not aligned (another form of tolerance), people lose trust and often feel unsafe. When the expectations are different for people without reason or reasoning, trust diminishes, culture is lost and your people will withhold everything you desire from them.

Admittedly, this topic—different standards—is being considered differently today due to the COVID pandemic and the many unique situations faced by team members. I recently heard a leader suggest that one key to leadership today and the future is flexibility—the willingness to treat people in different situations differently. However, this doesn't negate the truths about tolerance. The key is that tolerance creates unhealthy outcomes when it's not based on a reason the team is open to understand. The new realities of hybrid workforces will require leaders and organizations to consider certain policies, processes and expectations differently. In this new hybrid reality, we must also continue to be vigilant in assessing and addressing the tolerances that are having or likely to have a negative impact on your culture, team and organization.

I was recently facilitating a team retreat, and one of the top issues identified by a team member was the failure to enforce certain processes and procedures. When I asked the team member how this tolerance impacted her, she said, "I feel unsafe." That's a powerful emotion for a team member to experience, especially when other people say they should be allowed to do it their way because that's what they're used to. So often, we don't realize (hello … blind spot) how selfish and self-focused we're being when we insist on doing things our way, seemingly without caring about the impact it has on others and the message it communicates to others.

A few years ago, a partner in an accounting firm was complaining that many of their employees were slow in submitting their billed time (a critical issue in terms of billings, collections and cash flow). However, this partner was one of the worst offenders, and everyone knew it. While the partner felt he could choose not to comply with the process (because he was a partner), everyone else was expected to comply. It's no surprise that team members would fail to comply with expectations when they see others not complying (especially leaders). Frankly, if you believe that you as a leader can ignore the policies and procedures but expect everyone else to comply, you're missing what it means to be a leader. While there may be some legitimate exceptions, those exceptions and the reasons behind them must be clearly communicated and understood by the entire team.

For example, when I owned my law firm many years ago, our employees had regular office hours, but the lawyers didn't. The reason was simple—we expected the lawyers to do what had to be done to meet client needs and firm expectations, which often meant coming in early, working late or working at home. We didn't have the same expectations of our non-lawyer employees. We also clearly communicated this to the team and explained the reasons for the different expectations. Fortunately, we'd built a high level of trust, and everyone understood the reasons for the different expectations. Another key factor was that we (the professionals) consistently treated our non-lawyer team members with dignity and respect and as highly valued team members. This allowed us to have a culture where we worked as a team, had each other's backs and the team was highly engaged and committed to the firm's success.

I have no doubt that you're very aware of the people, situations and actions you're tolerating, however, you may not yet be fully aware of the negative impacts of these tolerances on your team, organization and outcomes. In the next section, I'll share with you a tolerance assessment process to help you navigate your tolerance factor differently going forward. For now, I offer you this simple reminder about tolerance—*what and who you tolerate are not exceptions to your culture and expectations … **they ARE your culture and expectations**—*and the impacts of this tolerance are the primary reason that your team, organizations and outcomes are not what you desire.

One way to visualize this impact is to envision that you've built a high-performance automobile that has every feature you need to accelerate and achieve your objectives. You've streamlined it, you've added many innovations and you've filled it with the highest quality fuel, and yet you're not achieving the speeds and outcomes you desire. Now, look behind you, and you'll see a heavy chain attached to the automobile and at the end of the chain is an anchor. An anchor that you're dragging behind you, slowing you down, damaging the automobile and the reason for all your challenges. That anchor is your tolerance factor and you must directly address it in order to alter your outcomes. Make no mistake about it, this will require shaking up your thinking, your communications, your relationships and your leadership. And yes, it involves taking risks, but these risks are essential in order to reduce and hopefully eliminate your tolerance factor so that you can achieve your desired outcomes.

## THE TOLERANCE ASSESSMENT PROCESS

I'm confident that you immediately identified many of the people (who) and situations (what) that you've been tolerating. I'm also certain that you'll be able to identify more if you invest a little bit of time and thought into the question. There will likely be some areas of tolerance that you'll initially miss because we've all gotten so good at rationalizing our tolerances under the category of good "reasons" (aka excuses). While you may be immediately aware of certain tolerances, I've discovered that who and what we tolerate is often covered up, and I also know that we rarely (if ever) fully assess our tolerances.

As I started sharing these concepts around tolerance and tolerance factors, I realized that I was leaving people hanging without a solution (other than just stopping it). This wasn't fair, so I developed a process for thoroughly assessing your tolerances and making new decisions about what and who you are tolerating. Even more important, we must make new and more conscious decisions around our tolerances, which is why I developed the tolerance assessment process, which consists of the following:

1. Assess the tolerance
2. Assess the impact
3. Assess the risks
4. Assess the win
5. Consciously choose
6. Let it go

In the rest of this chapter, we're going to walk through each of these assessment elements so that in the end, you'll be in a position to deeply understand your tolerances, the reasons for them and be in a great position to make a new decision about each of your tolerances. The key to this process is total honesty to yourself and everyone else involved in this process (hint: it's important to include others). You'll also understand your tolerances from new perspectives and depths, and these shifts will transform the ways you look at tolerance and tolerance impact.

First, you must assess tolerance, which is about honesty and clarity. Rather than generally labeling a person or situation, you must be clear and specific about what exactly you're tolerating. Here are some examples of tolerance descriptions that aren't clear:

* Sally is a bad employee
* Joe is an underperformer
* The team is not working well together
* Sam is a poor communicator
* Not everyone is following this process
* We're inconsistent about our hiring practices
* Jim is a bully
* Ellen is too direct
* Our meetings aren't run well
* People aren't following the vacation policy

Hopefully you get the point and can easily see how these descriptions, while simple, aren't helpful in assessing the tolerance and all of the remaining steps in the tolerance assessment process.

In contrast and to track the bad examples above, the following are examples of being clear regarding what and who you're tolerating:

- Sally talks behind people's back
- Joe is not meeting his sales quotas
- The team doesn't do well at direct communication and critical conversations
- Sam is distracted, doesn't listen well and often interrupts others
- The sales group is not following the expense report process
- We allow people to schedule interviews without working with the HR department
- Jim is verbally abusive of employees
- Ellen lacks emotional intelligence and empathy
- Our meetings don't start or finish on time
- Team members are allowed to take vacation time without consulting with HR

You'll see below why this tolerance clarity is so important but remember for now that tolerances and the potential solutions depend upon being honest and clear about exactly what and who is being tolerated. Otherwise, each of the following elements of the process will be negated or diluted.

The next step in this honesty journey is to clearly and specifically assess the current impact of the tolerance. In other words, what's the cost of the tolerance? Certainly, there's likely to be an impact on the effectiveness and efficiency of the team and organization, and these impacts ultimately mean lowered revenues and / or profits even if there's no direct causal link with the tolerance. While this impact is important to recognize, the people and culture impacts are often even more devastating and it's important to be specific in assessing the tolerance impact.

While there will always be nuances of the people and culture impacts, the common impacts nearly always include trust, engagement, communication, teamwork, collaboration, innovation and psychological safety. If not everyone has to follow the stated policies and processes, trust is broken and team members disconnect. When team members perceive that other team members get special treatment, they won't support each other, and silos spring up throughout the organization. When people are allowed to engage in behavior that doesn't align with the stated culture and values, then people conclude (for a great reason) that the culture and values aren't authentic. And as noted above, whatever and whoever is tolerated defines the culture and values of the organization, they're not just exceptions without impact.

*Whatever and whoever is tolerated defines the culture and values of the organization.*

While assessing the impact seems obvious, the critical emphasis here is to make sure the impact assessments are specific. This is important for two reasons. First, specificity is required in order to assess possible solutions and tolerance adjustments. Second, specificity is vital for the next two elements of the tolerance assessment process.

Once you're clear on the tolerance and its impact, you move on to honestly assessing the risks of potential tolerance changes, adjustments or eliminations. Once again, you must be clear and specific in identifying these potential risks, and yes, I said potential. The truth is that the risks of making changes in your tolerance are always potential since no one can predict the outcomes of those changes. This is an important distinction since we often assume that the potential risks are specific outcomes, but this risk assessment must assess not only the potential risks but the likelihood of those risks actually occurring.

In many cases, the go-to risk is that the people being tolerated will choose to either leave the organization (thereby losing the value you believe they bring) or their performance and value will be reduced even if they stay with the organization. While this risk must be considered, you must also balance this risk against the negative impact of the tolerance assessed in the prior step. It's easy to rationalize tolerance as critical to the organization's success, but we all know that no one person determines your success. We also know that tolerance impacts can often lead to toxic outcomes and cultures.

Another typical risk category is relational, such as the example above where one partner tolerated his partner's abusive behavior partly because they're brothers. Even if you're not dealing with family, there are always relationship risks (i.e., the fear of not being liked) when you ask people to be accountable to and in alignment with your expectations of others.

The most important risk consideration is the reality that tolerance impacts don't lower the bar in your organization, they ARE your bar. They also define your culture rather than being merely cultural impacts. Once you recognize this truth, you'll begin to more clearly see the ways that tolerance is what's holding your team and your organization back from achieving your objectives, building your desired culture and achieving your objectives in a timely fashion.

Admittedly, you may have already considered some of the prior elements of the tolerance assessment process, however, the next element is often ignored when you're considering tolerance and tolerance impacts. This essential element is assessing the likely wins (improvement opportunities) if you eliminate or minimize the tolerance.

Certainly, one win is eliminating or reducing the negative impacts of the tolerance (see Step 2 discussion above), but the potential wins don't end there. There are typically additional wins, benefits and opportunities that you'll experience when you make adjustments in the tolerance. Think of it this way—if you have a particular process designed to improve the organization's and team's performance, the existing tolerance will certainly negate these improvements. When you adjust the tolerance, then these negative performance impacts are reduced or eliminated. However, when you factor in all the other elements of tolerance impact, there's typically a multiplier effect in performance, opportunities and outcomes. This is the greatest opportunity when you choose to make tolerance adjustments in your organization.

We all know that when we discuss tolerance issues in your organization (even if you don't use the word tolerance), the conversations typically focus on three things: 1. General descriptions of the behavior that's outside expectations and values 2. Emotions around these behaviors 3. The risks associated with making changes in the tolerance (this is the land of rationalizations and excuses). We rarely talk about the wins that will come from adjusting the tolerance, which keeps us from fully and honestly assessing the tolerance, impacts, risks and rewards. This is why the assessing the wins step is likely the most important of all the assessment steps.

Now we come to the truest leadership step in this process—making a more conscious decision about the tolerance. Even after you honestly and openly engage in this tolerance process, you may choose not to make any tolerance adjustments, however, by engaging in the tolerance assessment process, you'll be in a position to make a more conscious and fully informed decision on what to do about the existing tolerances. I call this the leadership step because as a leader, being more conscious is perhaps the most important element of your leadership growth journey.

As a coach working with my clients, my goal is not necessarily to change leaders' decisions but to help leaders be more conscious in their leadership and make more conscious decisions. If you choose not to make any tolerance adjustments, you'll at least make that decision with full knowledge and understanding of the tolerance, the impacts, the risks and the wins. I must add that if you choose not to make any tolerance adjustments, I highly encourage you to consider having an honest conversation with everyone that's impacted by the tolerance.

Wherever you have tolerance issues, your people know it and have already made assumptions about it. The three most typical assumptions are that you're ignoring it, unaware of it or don't care about the ways the tolerance impacts the organization, team and performance. They also often assume that you haven't seriously considered the tolerance and its impacts, and this assumption causes an additional negative impact. While it might be a challenging conversation, communicate your decision to your people and give your honest reasons if you're choosing to continue to tolerate something or someone. Your people may not like the decision but they're more likely to respect you and your process, thereby minimizing but never eliminating some of the tolerance impacts.

The final step in the tolerance assessment process is the simplest but often the most difficult. Once you've made your tolerance decision (whatever that decision is), let it go. This means you stop talking about it and complaining about it. Once you've gone through the process, it's important that everyone stops discussing the tolerance issues unless and until you decide to make another intentional pass at the tolerance process. While people may not be happy, especially if the tolerance is allowed to continue, the ongoing conversations about something you've fully addressed and decided to continue tolerating take an additional toll on the organization, culture and trust. It's these ongoing conversations that represent a different form of toxic and limiting communication.

In other words, once you decide, the arguments, the discussions and the complaints must stop. Leadership requires decisiveness and once a conscious decision has been made, it's time to move on unless and until there's new information or you have a different awareness regarding the tolerance that requires that you undertake another tolerance assessment process. If you feel yourself or your team getting sucked back into the tolerance wormhole, just remember to let it go and move on.

## THE TOLERANCE ANCHOR

There's nothing complicated about the tolerance assessment process, but continuously utilizing it is vital to protect and preserve your culture and your performance. As I shared above, tolerance (sometimes called your tolerance factor) is the anchor that's holding back your leadership, team, culture and performance, and you can never fully accelerate and achieve unless and until you remove or at least minimize your tolerance anchor.

Yes, continue to look for ways to sharpen your saw as a leader and organization with perspective shifts and behavior changes outlined in this book, but never forget to invest in addressing your tolerance factor. This is the biggest obstacle to your leadership and desired outcomes, and it's also the arena that typically invokes the most fears about making tolerance adjustments. But as we now know, leadership is about taking risks, facing our fears and stepping into the fires of each leadership moment.

In the context of snow globe leadership, tolerance may require the greatest amount of shaking, shifting and disruption since tolerances are often deeply embedded in the culture and fabric of a team and organization. Thus, it will take more consistent and vigorous shaking to break loose the many tolerances that have become almost institutionalized in your organization. Tolerance shake ups can often be messy, and they're filled with uncertainty, but this is where leaders step up and leadership must shine—in the midst of the chaos, uncertainty and fear of the unknown. As we close this chapter, I ask you to ponder this simple question: What is and what will be your tolerance legacy as a leader?

# Chapter 13

# Actionizing Your Leadership

THERE YOU HAVE it—foundational perspective shifts, essential mindsets and critical tools to enhance, empower and energize your leadership and leadership impact. All disruptive, all impactful and all triggered and enabled by your willingness to vulnerably shake things up by shaking your snow globe and encouraging others to shake their own snow globes.

The old ways of leading and the loss of focus on the people-side of leadership have created a massive leadership gap—in fact, a leadership chasm—that must be closed for the good of our organizations, teams, people, relationships and world. Closing this chasm will not be accomplished by safely standing on this side and hoping for closure, but by boldly leaping across the divide and inspiring others to follow you. This is the essence of influence and the heart of leadership.

The need for transformational change in leadership is great and the urgency is even greater. The world is waiting for brave and bold leaders to take the risks of leading in these different and people-focused ways. The question is not whether new leadership is needed, but whether you'll be one of these new leaders. The question is not whether you have the necessary leadership position or permission, but whether you're willing to step up your leadership wherever you are—leading with or without position. The question is not whether leadership is about people, but whether you'll choose to lead with your eyes and heart focused on growing and building your people.

These unique, uncertain and sometimes chaotic times have further highlighted the scale of the leadership gap and clarified the people-impact of our leadership failures. More than ever, leadership is not only needed, *but leadership is the answer to the challenges we face today in every part of our businesses and lives*. My deepest desire is that you will be one of these brave and bold leaders to answer this call, and this leadership call for new action must include these new perspectives, mindsets and tools. This is the essence of actionizing your leadership.

The past two years have crystalized and amplified the need for disruptive leadership, and this disruption requires the types and nature of snow globe shaking that we've been discussing throughout this book. And this shaking must be followed by fundamental shifts in our thinking, perspectives, decisions and actions lest we fall victim to the same fate as the snow globe—vigorous shaking followed by swift settling. The critical message is communicated on the cover of this book … *shaken, not settled*. Mere shaking is not enough but it's the starting point, and this shaking must be accompanied by actionizing all these new ways of thinking, experiencing, seeing, communicating and relating.

I've always been drawn to and inspired by these profound words from Jungian analyst, consultant and author Robert Moore:

> "Could it be that in the twenty-fifth century, some elder historian is going to be telling stories? He's going to say that it came to pass that in the later years of the twentieth century, a small band of [people] of different races, from different walks of life, woke up. They looked around and

they saw what time it was and knew how desperate the situation was and how bad the odds were that they could do the work that needed to be done. Nevertheless, they said yes to this challenge, and children, though we cannot remember their names, we are eternally grateful to them." [35]

Talk about a call to action? The same can be said about the need for all of us to wake up, take risks and do the leadership work that needs to be done for the good of all. To look around, see how desperate the situation is, experience how great the need of the people is for new and different leadership and do what must be done to transform leadership and your leadership impact.

Make no mistake about it—people, teams, organizations, families and communities are waiting for you to step up your leadership. The question is not whether you can be one of the ones, but WILL you choose to be one of the ones. One of the brave ones. One of the bold ones. One of the courageous ones. One of the disruptive ones. One of the committed ones. One of the vulnerable ones. One of the shifting ones. One of the impactful ones.

This book is about shaking, and it's intended to perform the act of shaking up your thinking and perspectives. Ultimately, my hope and prayer is that this book will inspire you to shake up and shift your beliefs and actions so that you can transform your leadership, life, relationships and experience.

Where do you need to shake things up in your leadership or life? What situation requires a shake and a fresh look? What relationships need to be shaken up for the benefit of both parties? What plan needs to be adjusted and shaken up so you can clearly see what's working and what's not working once everything settles? If you want more magic in your life, then invite that magic by borrowing from the magic of snow globes. And remember this: *you've got to shake things to change things!*

# Endnotes

1   Harter, J (2020 February 4), *4 Factors Driving Record-High Employee Engagement in U.S., Retrieved August 21, 2021 from* https://www.gallup.com/workplace/284180/factors-driving-record-high-employee-engagement.aspx

2   *Id.*

3   Harter, J (2021 February 26) *U.S. Employee Engagement Rises Following Wild 2020, Retrieved August 21, 2021 from* https://www.gallup.com/workplace/330017/employee-engagement-rises-following-wild-2020.aspx

4   Ratanjee, V (2021 January 15) *Why Managers Need Leadership Development Too, Retrieved August 21, 2021 from* https://www.gallup.com/workplace/328460/why-managers-need-leadership-development.aspx

5   Jeff Nischwitz, interview with Larry English, May 13, 2020, in *Remote By Choice: Building a Great Virtual Organization*, Leadership Junkies Podcast Episode 15, produced by Craig Mathews, MP3 audio, 8:07, https://podcasts.apple.com/us/podcast/leadership-junkies-podcast/id1503936554?i=1000474498507

6   Jeff Nischwitz, interview with Lee Chambers, August 5, 2020, in *To Lead Is To Be Human: What You Need to Know to Lead Today*, Leadership Junkies Podcast Episode 39, produced by Craig

Mathews, MP3 audio, 26:50, https://podcasts.apple.com/us/podcast/leadership-junkies-podcast/id1503936554?i=1000487258041

7   Jeff Nischwitz, interview with Tommy Spaulding, June 3, 2020, in *Put Your Whole Heart In: Achieving Unprecedented Results Through Servant Leadership*, Leadership Junkies Podcast Episode 21, produced by Craig Mathews, MP3 audio, 8:29, https://podcasts.apple.com/us/podcast/leadership-junkies-podcast/id1503936554?i=1000476755362

8   *Id.* at 11:34.

9   *Id.* at 12:28.

10  Zak, P (2017 January – February) *The Neuroscience of Trust: Management Behaviors That Foster Employee Engagement, Retrieved August 21, 2021 from* https://hbr.org/2017/01/the-neuroscience-of-trust

11  Vulnerability is "a shortcut to trust." *Id.* Endnote 5.

12  *Id.*

13  Brown, Brene. "Power of Vulnerability." *TED: Ideas Worth Spreading*, June 2010 https://www.ted.com/talks/brene_brown_the_power_of_vulnerability

14  Brown, Brene. "Listening to Shame." *TED: Ideas Worth Spreading*, March 2012 https://www.ted.com/talks/brene_brown_listening_to_shame.

15  *Id.* at 5:08 of transcript.

16  *Id.* at 3:39 of transcript.

17  Jeff Nischwitz, interview with Walt Rakowich, September 28, 2020 in *Transparency Wins: The Vital Role of Transparency in Building Trust and Transformational Influence*, Leadership Junkies Podcast Episode 54, produced by Craig Mathews, MP3 audio, 12:21, https://podcasts.apple.com/us/podcast/leadership-junkies-podcast/id1503936554?i=1000492885749

18 Brown, Brene. "Listening to Shame" TED Talk at 3:39 of transcript.

19 *Id*. Endnote 17 at 34:20-35:44.

20 Jeff Nischwitz, *Just One Step: Walking Backwards to the Present on the Camino Trail* (Eagle Heart Press 2020), Chapter 15 at 189-190.

21 *Id*. Endnote 17 at 39:37-41:13.

22 https://www.osha.gov/aboutosha

23 *See* Faville, K (2021 July 15) *According to Mental Health Index: Elevated Risk of PTSD Continues; Adversely Impacts Employee Stress Levels, Resilience and Cognition, Retrieved September 15, 2021 from* https://apnews.com/press-release/pr-newswire/business-health-coronavirus-pandemic-mental-health-stress-3362372ccb2050702 a05dba28e48bce5 for a discussion of the psychological impact of the pandemic in the workplace, including potential PTSD impacts.

24 Simon Sinek, *Leaders Eat Last: Why Some Teams Pull Together and Others Don't* (Penguin 2014), 26-27.

25 Sinek, Simon "Why Good Leaders Make You Feel Safe" *TED: Ideas Worth Spreading*, March 2014 https://www.ted.com/talks/simon_sinek_why_good_leaders_make_you_feel_safe? at Transcript 4:50-5:04.

26 *Id*. Transcript at 6:10-6:19.

27 Vuleta, B (2021 March 30) *30 Remarkable Stats About Millennials in the Workplace, Retrieved August 31, 2021 from* https://whattobecome.com/blog/millennials-in-the-workplace.

28 See employee engagement discussion and Gallup data in Chapter 1.

29 DiJulius, J (2021 August 30) *The Great Resignation – Employees Are Quitting at Record Rates, Retrieved September 15, 2021 from* https://thedijuliusgroup.com/the-great-resignation-employees-are-quitting-at-record-rates

30 Hoppa, L (2021 August 18) Association for Talent Development, *The Great Resignation Continues to Elevate Our Need for Humanity*

*at Work, Retrieved September 30, 2021 from* https://www.td.org/atd-blog/the-great-resignation-continues-to-elevate-our-need-for-humanity-at-work

31  *Id.* Endnote 25 at Transcript 9:56-10:28.

32  *Id.* at Endnote 7.

33  No Mud, No Lotus, Parallax Press 2014, 23.

34  *Id.* at 75.

35  Moore PhD, R (1995 July 17), *Masculine Initiation for the 21st Century: Facing the Challenge of a Global Brotherhood, Retrieved September 7, 2021 from* https://www.crossroadscounselingchicago.com/wp-content/uploads/2013/03/Reclaiming-Sacred-Masculine.pdf at 18.

# Acknowledgements

This snow globe metaphor for leadership and life hit me like a lightning bolt on a stage in Raleigh, NC several years ago, and it's been at the forefront of my work and messages ever since. And yet this book wasn't even on my radar until my incredible speaker's mastermind group (MasterMind 500) asked me this question in early 2021: "Everything you speak, coach and train about is based upon the theme of shaking things up, disrupting thinking and leading differently—snow globe leadership—why haven't you written that book yet?" This is the beauty and challenge of a mastermind group—seeing the things I'm missing and asking the questions that need to be asked (and answered).

I'm immensely grateful to the MasterMind 500 for supporting me when I'm uncertain, challenging me when I'm off course and believing in me always. Thank you Stan Phelps, Marcey Rader, Justin Jones-Fosu, Kevin Snyder and David Rendall for lovingly coaxing this book out of me.

I'm also grateful for the thousands of people with whom I've shared the snow globe leadership message with over the past few years, many of whom have shared with me the impact that this disruptive message had on them and their leadership. I'm also grateful for the many people who've let me know that the snow globe leadership message—shaking things up and never settling—has stuck with them, inspired them and guided them both personally and professionally. You've all provided me with unimaginable support and the courage to keep shaking, shifting and sharing.

I also want to thank my Network Professional, Inc. (NPI) "family" in Tampa. Your support and encouragement have meant the world to me as I've walked this journey of writing and birthing *Snow Globe Leadership*. I look forward to continuing to share our business growth journey.

As with all my books, I'm deeply grateful for the friends, clients, partners, podcast hosts, connections and conversations I've had over the past few years. So many people, presentations, interviews, questions and interactions have helped me to define, refine, expand and enhance the snow globe leadership concept, message and lessons. I've long been drawn to Proverbs 27:17—"iron sharpens iron"—and I'm grateful for the many people, experiences and interactions that have helped sharpen the concepts in this book and me.

I also want to thank Jamie Morlock for allowing me the space to write this book, for encouraging me, for her curiosity and interest and for her questions along the way. Her support was invaluable on this journey.

Finally, I'm grateful for the encouragement, support and nudges from Liza Marie Garcia and NOW Publishing. I met Liza soon after I moved to the Tampa Bay area, and I was immediately drawn to her entrepreneurial journey and her passion for publishing. When it was time to decide who to partner with for the publication of *Snow Globe Leadership*, the answer was swift and clear, and I've loved working with Liza and her team to bring this book to life.

With Love and Gratitude!

Jeff Nischwitz
October 15, 2021

# The Leadership Junkies Podcast
# (https://leadershipjunkies.com)

*Proud Partner of Evergreen Podcasts Network*

Leadership Growth * Business Growth * Personal Growth * Revenue Growth

*Transforming businesses, organizations, teams, relationships, communities and lives, one leadership ripple at a time.*

Jeff Nischwitz is the Co-Creator, Co-Host and Chief Question Officer of the Leadership Junkies Podcast, which is on a mission to change the heart of leadership and provide implementable ideas that leaders everywhere can use to grow themselves, their teams and their businesses. The Leadership Junkies are also committed to empowering everyday leaders to step up, lean in and take the risk of leading wherever they are, without position and permission.

The Leadership Junkies believe that there are four differences between good versus thriving organizations:

1. **Leadership**—It's clear that there's a growing leadership gap. While there are some good managers and a few who do well at running their business, the evidence shows that we're failing at building strong teams and growing and developing our people. In other words, too many businesses are surviving rather than thriving.

2. **People First**—Leadership has always been and will always be about people—building trust, empowering people, inspiring influence and creating collaborative impact as a team. When leaders and organizations commit to and invest in growing their people, they reduce costs, increase engagement, improve execution, amplify profits and accelerate growth. When you put your people first in words and action, you create the secret sauce for a thriving and sustainable business.

3. **Impact Attention and Awareness**—Most people's issues in organizations are in some way the result of a lack of impact attention and awareness. While most organizations have goals, the true objective for great organizations is impact—impact for our clients, our team and the community. In order to create impact, you must be committed to growing your impact attention, and awareness.

4. **Think and Do Different**—Too many leaders and organizations continue to do business, solve problems and pursue opportunities the same way they've been doing for many years. The world (and the workforce) has changed, and this is no longer a viable

approach. We share unique and disruptive ideas and interview guests to help our listeners think differently and to do things differently. This involves shaking things up *and* shifting our perspectives and actions while we're shaking.

Welcome to the Leadership Junkies Podcast … ***a new way of living, leading and impacting!***

jeffnischwitz
Transforming People & Organizations
...one truth at a time

Facilitator of Truth ... Accelerator ... Relationship Builder ... Master Storyteller ... Chief Inquisitor ... Story Debunker ... Disruptor ... Transformational Coach ... Inspirational Model for Change ... and *Snow Globe Shaker!* This is how business leaders and clients describe Jeff Nischwitz.

Jeff is the Founder of The Nischwitz Group, a speaking, consulting and coaching company that transforms people and organizations—*one truth at a time!* With people and relationships, perception IS the only reality and the moment we shift our perceptions and actions, we immediately shift our experiences and outcomes.

As an international keynote speaker and master facilitator, Jeff energizes audiences and challenges people to shake things up in their leadership, businesses and lives. Jeff's audiences experience disruptive thinking, challenging questions, vulnerable sharing and inspired perspectives on the path to achieving more impact and influence through and throughout life—an experience that's been called "Getting Jeffed!"

As a transformational business and leadership coach, Jeff disrupts people's thinking and perspectives in order to accelerate and grow their leadership, teams, businesses and impact. Often challenging, Jeff is a master inquisitor with the rare ability to ask questions that go beyond the heart of the matter, into the soul of a person and even an organization. So skilled and intuitive are Jeff's questions, that his seemingly innocent inquiry, "Do you mind if I ask you a question?", often comes with a warning: Be careful before you say yes, because you may learn, experience or uncover something that you were not expecting … and perhaps something you've never seen or known before. This is just one of the many gifts that Jeff brings to the people and organizations that are ready for transformational change.

In addition to speaking and coaching, Jeff consistently delivers impact to his clients in many ways:

1. **In-House Training**—Delivering in-house training to organizations on leadership, team engagement, building culture, communication, feedback and accountability, as well as in-house training for professionals (lawyers, accountants and financial services) on business development and relationship building. Jeff's also developed a niche in working with construction, architecture and engineering firms to help them empower and enhance their business presentations and client pitches.

2. **Leadership Development**—A structured leadership development program that can be implemented across a group of existing or future leaders within any organization.

3. **Facilitation**—Facilitating sessions for organizations around strategic planning, team retreats, ideation sessions or some strategic initiative.

Jeff works with a wide range of organizations on growing leaders, building engaged and empowered teams, accountability and achieving a whole other level of impact and influence. Some niches include legal, accounting, banking and financial services, construction, architecture, engineering, technology and family businesses.

Jeff is the author of four other books:

*Think Again! Innovative Approaches to the Business of Law* (American Bar Association 2007), which offers creative and practical advice on building an exceptional law firm.

*Unmask: Let Go of Who You're "Supposed" to Be & Unleash Your True Leader* (Motivational Press 2014), a road map for navigating your own personal journey as a leader in your business, career, relationships and life.

*Arrows of Truth: Simple Shifts for Personal Transformation* (Eagle Heart Press 2016), a workbook style practical guide for creating real change in your life, relationships and leadership.

*Just One Step: Walking Backwards to the Present* (Eagle Heart Press 2020), the story of Jeff's 200-mile walk on the Camino de Santiago in Spain and a guide for people and leaders who want to live and lead with more confidence, less stress and more impact.

To learn and explore more, visit www.nischwitzgroup.com.

# About the Author

Jeff Nischwitz is the Founder and Chief Snow Globe Shaker of The Nischwitz Group, an organization he created in 2009 with a simple mission – transform leaders and leadership to create more conscious, intentional and positive impact in organizations, teams, families, communities and lives. Jeff's also the co-host of the Leadership Junkies Podcast (https://leadershipjunkies.com) and co-founder of Cardivera, a leadership development training and development ecosystem for growing leaders, people and businesses.

Jeff's known as many things including facilitator of truth, relationship builder, master storyteller, chief question officer, story debunker and noticer. Naturally curious, especially about people, Jeff's always bringing a unique question, perspective or insight to situations, opportunities and challenges. Jeff's known for his vulnerability, presence, authenticity and, of course, his infamous hugs.

Over the past 37 years, Jeff's professional, business and entrepreneurial path has been quite the journey. Beginning as a successful lawyer, Jeff left the corporate law firm where he was a partner to take the leap into entrepreneurship by creating his own law firm. After building and growing that firm, Jeff did what few dare to even consider: *he left that which he knew and which was successful to go in search of his true calling.* For Jeff, getting by or merely succeeding without loving what he does was not acceptable. For Jeff, getting by or merely succeeding without loving what he does was not acceptable.

Like many entrepreneurs, Jeff's journey had many twists, turns and yes, stumbles, which Jeff openly shares and speaks on as part of his authentic story telling—the good, the bad and sometimes the ugly. When asked how he transitioned from entrepreneurial lawyer to international speaker and transformation coach, Jeff is famous for the following:

> I'd love to tell you that it was a great plan, brilliantly executed but it's more like a car wreck where the car rolled over several times and somehow landed on its wheels. I was injured and even had some broken bones, but I was alive and the car was still drivable. So I took off in the direction it was pointing and I've been going ever since."

After several years of trying to fit in to the traditional corporate and business world, Jeff once again leapt into his true life when he founded *The Nischwitz Group.* Jeff now helps entrepreneurs and owners to grow and accelerate their businesses, teams, impact and lives.

Jeff grew up in Dayton, OH and graduated from Ohio Northern University (B.S. Business Administration). He later received his J.D. degree from the Ohio State University College of Law, and then headed to Cleveland, OH to start his legal career. Jeff now lives in Tampa, FL, but considers the world is oyster both for business and travel adventures.

Jeff has been actively involved with the Mankind Project International (https://mankindproject.org) since 2010; now as a certified co-leader facilitating men's retreats around the country and world. The Mankind Project is a non-profit organization that offers transformational trainings, workshops and programs to help men show up differently in their lives, relationships and leadership. Jeff is also the Chair of the Board of Wounded Healers International (https://woundedhealersintl.org), an organization committed to increasing awareness and understanding around sexual violence prevention, manifestation and supporting survivors by offering and financially supporting programs to educate, support and empower both girls and boys towards building a culture of mutual respect.

Jeff is the proud father of his two adult sons, Eric and Kyle. When he's not living his passion as a national speaker and transformation coach, you'll likely find him exploring Civil War battlefields or other historical locations with his Dad, dipping his toes into an ocean, lake or river, or exploring new cities and areas across the country and the world. He's also known for his love of bold red wines, cigars, hearty bourbon, Broadway theater and hanging out while enjoying genuine conversations.